Teach Like a Human

Teach Like a Human

Essays for Parents and Teachers

Miriam Hirsch

ROWMAN & LITTLEFIELD
Lanham • Boulder • New York • London

Published by Rowman & Littlefield
An imprint of The Rowman & Littlefield Publishing Group, Inc.
4501 Forbes Boulevard, Suite 200, Lanham, Maryland 20706
www.rowman.com

6 Tinworth Street, London SE11 5AL, United Kingdom

British Library Cataloguing in Publication Information Available

Library of Congress Cataloging-in-Publication Data

Names: Hirsch, Miriam, 1968– author.
Title: Teach like a human : essays for parents and teachers / Miriam Hirsch.
Description: Lanham : Rowman & Littlefield, [2020] | Includes bibliographical references and index.
 | Summary: "Written for parents and teachers this is a collection of essays focused on educating children to care about themselves, their communities, and the world we share"— Provided by publisher.
Identifiers: LCCN 2020010341 (print) | LCCN 2020010342 (ebook) | ISBN 9781475857214 (cloth) | ISBN 9781475857238 (epub)
Subjects: LCSH: Education, Humanistic. | Moral education. | Education—Parent participation.
Classification: LCC LC1011 .H53 2020 (print) | LCC LC1011 (ebook) | DDC 370.11/2—dc23
LC record available at https://lccn.loc.gov/2020010341
LC ebook record available at https://lccn.loc.gov/2020010342

To my husband, David Hirsch

Contents

Preface

This is not the preface I thought I would write: COVID-19 has changed everything. Teaching went online, parenting went 24/7, and work/home boundaries dissolved routines, schedules, and professional personas. The shifts have affected mental health, social-emotional stability, career growth, and basically planning anything. In sum, the future doesn't bear as much similarity to the past as it once did.

The questions that encompass teaching likewise poke holes in taken for granted ways of knowing and doing. Do we prepare teachers exclusively for teaching in remote online classrooms or continue to think of physical environments and synchronous instruction? Should parents assume more responsibility for social skill development and relationship-building practices because conflict resolution and collaboration in distance-learning contexts do not clearly support meaningful behavioral change?

The questions persist and the uncertainties grow. The anxiety is confusing and challenging for all people of all ages. At the end of the day, what can we do but teach like a human, full of hope, full of fear, full of doubt, full of drive, and full of love.

My favorite math problem comes from ninth grade geometry class and it goes something like this. . . .

If you cut two lengths of wood from one piece and then you compare the measurements, they are not the same. Why?

It stumped me as a ninth grader. I didn't know what the text was asking and it didn't seem like any other math problem that I had ever encountered.

The answer is sawdust.

This is the only math problem from K–12 mathematics instruction that I can recall vividly, and I have often considered it when I think about teaching like a human. There is always something small, subtle, and vitally important that is overlooked but affects change significantly. Whatever we do has an effect, and that effect influences something else. Ray Bradbury (1953/2008) plays with this message in his famous short story, "A Sound of Thunder." In the classic tale, the protagonist goes back in time, steps on a butterfly, and returns to a very different present. We are now in a very different present and we didn't even have to go back in time.

Choices narrow or expand opportunities. In learning, it is not only that every action has a reaction, but that every choice changes the learning environment. The point is the choices still matter. Teaching like a human still means relationships, smiles, generous but patient feedback, or, for example, the idea that birdsong trilling from an open window has the power to inform our consciousness, bring music to our soul, and inspire drawings, poetry, or the construction of a bird feeder. Teaching and learning will always matter, and parents and teachers need to partner to do this sacred work. May our choices anchor the growth of our children and students, and bring light, joy, and inspiration to the world they inherit.

Miriam Hirsch

July 2020

NOTE

Bradbury, R. (2008). "A Sound of Thunder." In *The golden apples of the sun & other stories* (pp. 113–26). Doubleday (originally published 1953).

Introduction

Educating children requires intelligence, compassion, creativity, and, above all, artistry. As Horace Mann (cited in Cremin, 1957, p. 21) reminds, "Teaching is the most difficult of all arts, the profoundest of all sciences." The push/pull tension between scientific research–based educational interventions and artistic intuition of teachable moments is a familiar struggle. In the early 1900s, John Dewey debunked either-or thinking that pitted traditional education against progressive education. Our current climate has returned to such illogical conflicts. High-stakes accountability measures and standards-based teaching strategies will never solve the problem of teaching all children according to their needs. Children need strong relationships, positive role models, good friends, and high expectations from people who care about helping them achieve. Physical, social, and emotional health are likewise important aspects of human development. *It truly all matters.* And, while research-based theory will not remediate every issue parents or teachers will face, theory does advance thinking and enable stronger choices. The situation is indeed daunting. As *Ethics of the Fathers* (2:21) states, "It is not up to you to complete the task, but you are not free to desist from it."

The purpose of this book is to illuminate how small moments with our children and students can matter in profound ways, and how parents and teachers can galvanize experiences and interactions to deepen character, insight, empathy, and joy in the people and things around us. To teach like a human means to teach with "wide-awakeness," the Maxine Greene term for the highest degree of consciousness. "The teacher herself has to be alive. The teacher herself can't come in the room with the problem of Hamlet already

1

solved. I think she has to come in with the same open questions, with the same wonder that children will feel" (Greene, 2012, p. 180).

To teach like a human means to keep in mind the deep responsibility of educators to raise the next generation to care about themselves, their communities, and the world around them.

> Why does that family of cardinals seem to return to our yard every year?
> Who makes up new words and how do words get retired?
> Why do I have to be the one to go over and be nice first?

This book focuses on qualitative aspects of human life for teachers and parents to nurture without surplus resources. Based on her work in an undergraduate preservice educator preparation program, K–12 teaching experience, mentoring new teachers, and lived experiences of childhood and childrearing, the author examines the craft of education and makes recommendations for how to think about pedagogy as the pursuit of humanity. This collection of essays reorients thinking about education for life not just for access to the next schooling tier. Education for life evokes John Dewey (1938/1977, p. 48): "The most important attitude that can be formed is that of desire to go on learning." And learning is never unidirectional; parents and teachers will need to consciously learn from children and students for learning to be successful.

Chapter 1, "The Mathematics of Mothering," explores how concepts from organizational theory like redundancy and satisficing (Simon, 1947) recontextualize parenting in our 24/7 world, with its constantly assaulting data stream. The chapter introduces ways of making sense of parenting today that reduce stress, anxiety, and guilt.

"The Parent as Curriculum Developer," chapter 2, introduces strategies parents can use to encourage children to strive for happiness. Self-destructive behaviors cross all socioeconomic, gender, and age categories, and parents need to remember that they are educating children not only to young adulthood, but also to set them up for managing happiness throughout the landscape of life.

Chapter 3, "Lessons from Mrs. Bird," demonstrates how interactions with children in nature (i.e., the bird builds a nest on the air conditioner) expand into authentic learning experiences, generating inquiry, reflection, and dialogue. It showcases how small events that grab children's attention can be seen as part of the larger process of cognitive development.

"Contending with Sibling Rivalry," chapter 4, draws insight from biblical sources to deepen perspective and sharpen tools for minimizing sibling rivalry. This chapter confronts foundational family dynamics that skew relationships and threaten familial bonds with mindsets and practices that enhance home and hearth.

Chapter 5, "'Reading Schools': A Primer," assists parents in the school selection process with tools to make sense of what they hear, see, and sense when they explore school organizations. This chapter includes key questions for parents to ask and identifies flags that warrant caution when faced with critical schooling decisions.

"Reclaiming the Art of Listening," chapter 6, attends to the aural component of the classroom and real life in three dimensions: listening to one's self, listening to others, and listening to the world. The influence of technology on the human capacity for attention requires calibration so the capacity to listen mindfully is not lost.

Chapter 7, "Out of the Box and Between the Lines," redefines creativity as a vital property of human expression throughout life. In this chapter, creativity is seen as part of every human endeavor, from running bases to plating desserts, adumbrated with core elements of discipline, feedback, and persistence.

"Sifting the Metaphor: 'Teaching as a Culinary Art,'" chapter 8, uses the lens of the culinary arts to see the profession of educator through a new perspective. This nuanced understanding of education deepens respect for the art and science of teaching, and upgrades the role of teacher as a professional.

Chapter 9, "'More Beauty in a Rock': What We Don't Teach and How It Matters," showcases the often-absent or misdirected skill of discernment. Exploring facets of curriculum in layman terms, this chapter asserts that the slow, careful qualitative skill of discernment can strengthen decision-making capacities and lifelong personal health and satisfaction.

"Teach like a Human: The Reality Gap in Teacher Preparation," chapter 10, challenges the current drive to mechanize teaching and learning. Teaching like a human, the title and overarching theme of the book, means using finely tuned human senses, intuition, and perceptive capacities to understand children more uniquely and particularly, something only a human can do.

The power of the home–school connection is often cited in the literature in terms of parent–teacher communication, building community, and reinforcing culturally responsive pedagogy. This work nudges the relationship in an alternative direction, asking both parents and teachers to invest deeply in each child by honoring the uniqueness of each and the time and place in which we live. Finances may improve education, but so will paying close attention to the child, his/her world, and the world we are privileged to share together.

REFERENCES

Cremin, L. (Ed.). (1957). *The republic and the school: Horace Mann on the education of free Man*. New York: Teachers College Press.

Dewey, J. (1938/1977). *Experience and education*. New York: Simon & Schuster. (Original work published in 1938.)

Greene, M. (2012). Rebellions, breakthroughs, and secret gardens: The arts and imagination. In H. Kohl & T. Oppenheim (Eds.), *The muses go to school: Inspiring stories about the importance of arts in education* (pp. 175–85). New York: The New Press.

Simon, H. (1947). *Administrative behavior*. New York: Macmillan.

Part I

For Parents (and Teachers)

Chapter One

The Mathematics of Mothering

SIX LESSONS FROM PRINCIPLES OF ORGANIZATIONAL
THEORY FOR PARENTS TO MASTER

The contemporary conundrum of work and family responsibilities in our 24/7 world of connectedness creates seemingly endless conflict. Answer the boss or respond to the teacher? Answer both too quickly and it will take three more e-mails to each to clarify what was meant and how it was meant. Parents today have a myriad of choices at different junctures in their lives, but they are constantly overwhelmed with major issues and minor details without any road map to ease the pressure of simultaneously advancing both aims, career and family. And, no matter how savvy or fit one becomes, there are still days when the shrill cry of the toddler moves sane people off-kilter, laundry overflows into the living room, and the refrigerator decides to stop working. Forget about what the neighbor does, how neat their children look, or why you forgot your sister's birthday again; it is time to move beyond comparison and competition. In addition, mothering is no longer exclusive to birth mom. Taking care of young like a mother would, mothering, is addressed by any individual who assumes this role, but it does not happen effectively without considerable energy and insight.

The field of organizational psychology offers different language and mentality to frame actions, thoughts, and feelings. Thinking about the family unit as an organization rather than the other end of a frustrating dilemma opens new understandings, implications, and inquiry. Let's say it is not work versus family but that the family is itself an organizational unit. This perspective shifts focus away from the individual as the role-bound hyperspazzed super-person and reinterprets family as a dynamic organization. It is not about semantics; it is about reconceiving notions of family and mothering through the lens of organizational life.

This chapter presents six lessons adapted from organizational theory and applied to mothering. The first step begins by debunking mothering as a purely intuitive natural response to children. Does anyone know what to do at all times for all children of all ages? Everyone is more proficient at some tasks than others, and learning new tips, insights, and approaches is part and parcel of life. This chapter is entitled "The Mathematics of Mothering" intentionally. Mathematics implies form, structure, and analytic thinking. In this way, the term *mathematics* can be seen as a set of tools generating both descriptive and predictive information about the subject of interest. As such, the term bolsters mothering with confidence, rigor, and wit. (Note: This is the class that should be offered in college.)

LESSON 1: AUTOBIOGRAPHY IS A BIASED ESTIMATOR

The generational divide between mothers and daughters, and fathers and sons (and mothers and sons, and fathers and daughters), is composed of a powerful paradox. On the one hand, there is no way on earth that individuals want to replicate ineffective or inefficient patterns from their parents. On the other hand, much of what is known or feels comfortable is the direct result of childhood experiences. This tension permeates and permutates throughout life; however, just because something was a) the most awful experience of one's life, b) the reason why the individual is what she/he is today, or c) the best decision ever made, this might not be the same for one's child. No matter how certain one is that something was good or bad, it seems wise to acknowledge the sentiment and then suspend its influence on parenting or teaching. Why?

The vast number of differences between the lives of parent and child precludes using autobiographical experience as a weighted factor in the mathematics of mothering. The child is living in a different sociocultural climate; different historical era; and different environmental, technological, and political landscape. These things matter. Yes, biology is pretty much a constant, but the psychological and social-emotional makeup of children does not align precisely in a one-to-one relationship with their parents. And as smart as one is, it is virtually impossible to truly understand the mindset of a child of any age. The older ones often claim, "That was then, this is now" or "It's not like that anymore." So do try to get into (understand) the head of one's child, but don't totally rely on the lens of autobiographical foci: This is sometimes the case of "Keep out to stay in."

LESSON 2: SATISFICING BALANCES THE EQUATION

Simon (1947) coined the term *satisficing* to explain how organizations have to be content with good-enough decisions. He explains that since people have to make decisions based on incomplete information to which they cannot attach accurate values or equally explore all options, decisions must be based on simple rules of thumb and a sense of bounded rationality. Parents know this principle intuitively: The home haircut with crooked bangs is good enough; the burnt cookies will be fine for the office party. Yet, there is an edgy strain of perfectionism attached to today's mothering. The constant prioritization of time conveys weight to the decision-making. Since this is the chosen path, to the exclusion of other demands on time, the task better be done well. Such pressure can develop into internal skirmishes of self-validation. Yet, if good enough is good enough for really big, powerful, and industrious organizations, why are parents still feeling badly about the child's home haircut and making another batch of cookies at midnight?

Satisficing is not about lowering expectations, "flaking" out of obligations, or shirking responsibilities. It is an honest acknowledgment of the limitations of the natural order of things. Things happen beyond our control, and people are not controllable. When children wake with a bad bout of stomach flu the night before a pivotal presentation, all is not lost. Satisfice, gather the relevant information, gather one's internal chi, and trust the process. Parents have to realize and internalize the ambiguity and quirkiness of the role. We live on the edge, but that should not make us edgy. Embrace the wonder of the unknown and the unknowable: "Hmm, this is not the way it was supposed to go . . . so okay." As a mentor of mine once advised, "Be curious, not furious." Push aside the frustration and stress of thwarted plans, allocated hours, and critical decisions. The challenge is to calm the angst of redirected energies by acknowledging imperfection, limitation, and flux: the very nature of the human condition.

LESSON 3: THE RETURN THEORY

Guess what . . . it's got to go back to the store (or Amazon). Yes, the application was filled out incorrectly. And the library book was left in the ladies' bathroom. Instead of feeling like a failure, what if there was an accepted understanding that 10% of the time things had to be redone or repeated? What if parents didn't think they had to do everything perfect from the first get-go? Let's say there was an agreement from the onset that about 10% of the time things went awry. Thus, when one returns from the store with the wrong size batteries or one treks to the mall leaving the savings coupon at home, it was just filling the individual's quota of the return theory obligation. In this way, innocent mistakes are not so personal or significant. Clearly, this is not in reference to life-or-death matters, just the nitty-gritty annoyances and contrivances of daily life, the mundane minutiae that cracks the core of any semisane parent.

Instead of thinking that the family will dissolve without the particular need met, it might be more helpful to view such repetition and edits as just part of the rules of the game. It could be a little less or a little more, but about 10% of the time, one is going to have to repeat, edit, adjust, review, or return something. It is just part of the process, built into the system. Get used to it, and don't fret about the process. In fact, it builds character.

LESSON 4: GENERATE REDUNDANCY

This one will save the parent time and time again. Now, despite the fact that, as discussed in the previous lessons, there are real limits on knowledge, control, and personality, successful organizations practice the generation of redundancy. Redundancy has dual citizenship. First, it has a built-in fail-safe mechanism that enables systems to keep operating despite mini-breakdowns or stoppages. Second, redundancy can also be thought of as excess capacity allowing for innovation and development (Morgan, 1997). Next, consider each in turn.

Redundancy is not only about buying copious amounts of tuna fish and paper towels at Costco. In the context of mothering, it is about assembling backup systems for carpooling, carrying the phone number of the pediatrician with you at all times, and teaching all family members how to make lunches. It is naive and inefficient to think that as a parent, one is indispensable and irreplaceable. Of course, one is, and, of course, one is not. The better the individual is at arranging contingency plans, the less harried one will be when something goes differently than anticipated.

Ironically enough, the complement to generating redundancy as a backing-up process is the germination of pockets of creativity and ingenuity. Eminent choreographer Twyla Tharp (2003) develops this theme in her book *The Creative Habit*. In this work, she exhorts the notion that discipline breeds structure for creative inspiration. She explains that when the major pieces of the game are in place, a mental and physical space on the space–time continuum opens up. When the systems are up and running efficiently, there is enough slack for spontaneous sparks of sublime inspiration. Suddenly there is room to breathe, reflect, revisit, and refine. This lesson moves beyond Tharp's plea for individual discipline to the larger playing field of family life. If one can generate redundancy, then there is a greater chance of keeping the systems running pretty smoothly more of the time. And if the major systems are operational, then openings have been created for new ideas, dreams, and goals to emerge. Needless to say, there is also time and space to carve out a place for the parent to do something for himself/herself with no guilt at all. Go for it.

LESSON 5: DEVALUE ALL-OR-NOTHING THINKING

The parent is not up to bat in the bottom of the ninth, bases loaded, two outs, with the team behind in the count. Wrong game. Mothering has more ambiguity surrounding the score. Managing paradox and embracing complexity more accurately describe family life on a daily basis. How does one make the lunches, fill out forms, find socks, remember the grocery list, and plan the birthday parties? The basement is flooding, the baby is soiled, and the school nurse is on the phone asking for lice-checking volunteers. The craziness of life simultaneously invigorates the soul and depletes resources. Do not add to this flow by impeding the flux and transformation with cognitive all-or-nothing blocks. "Either I tell him exactly how I feel or I keep it to myself" and "I already tried that and it did not work" are examples of this misguided way of thinking. Be creative, fluid, and persistent. All-or-nothing stunts growth, ingenuity, and drive. There is never only one way to do something.

Of course, this is not to say that firm discipline is not effective or important in the child-rearing process: That is an absolute dictum. This principle has to do with expanding repertoire and avoiding "getting stuck" in inefficient behavioral or mental patterns. "Hence the all-important message: Limit your thinking and you will limit your range of action" (Morgan, 1997, p. 351). It is important to remember that flexibility is not only about musculature; it is a disposition that diminishes stress.

LESSON 6: SLEEP IS AN EXPONENTIAL FACTOR

Intuitively, a well-rested person functions better, is better able to think on their feet, and can respond to children more sensitively and appropriately. Thus, if one can only do one thing today, getting a good night's sleep should be a top priority. Interestingly enough, Astros star pitcher Justin Verlander, age 36, aims for 10 hours a night (Wagner, 2019). Moreover, as the rush-rush nature of economic necessity presses aggressively into time allocation prioritization, there is an alarming tendency to complicate simple choices. We need an alternative between the frenzied multitasker and the worn-out caregiver. Clearly, there are times when rushing and running is the correct response, but one must ask if the bullet train is really leaving the station and the individual is behind schedule. People are smart, capable, creative, and interesting: If the only response to the situation is to shriek, then sleep may be the solution.

Sleep is a better palliative than caffeine or chocolate. Life is tough; raising children to be moral, responsible, and healthy individuals is a most noble and difficult task. There is no magic pathway suitable for everyone to follow. Some of these lessons will make intuitive sense, and others will seem ludicrous. Learn from what others do, but don't wallow in self-doubt, insecurity, or loneliness because someone does something better or differently. Stop comparing and competing. There is no ideal, there are only ideas.

The mathematics of mothering traces an infinity at both ends of the spectrum. The parent will never meet everyone's needs all the time. Nor will she/he always fail at finding the right thing to say or do. The point of the calculations and mental reckoning is to stretch and shrink the space of mothering so that it fits *you*, and you alone. But do remember, autobiographical experiences should not be the only resource under consultation. So, get some sleep, buy extra toilet paper, don't berate yourself for errors, and remember good enough is really . . . good . . . enough!

REFERENCES

Morgan, G. (1997). *Images of organization*. Thousand Oaks, CA: Sage.

Simon, H. (1947). *Administrative behavior*. New York: Macmillan.

Tharp, T. (2003). *The creative habit: Learn it and use it for life*. New York: Simon & Schuster.

Wagner, J. (2019, July 9). Justin Verlander: The Astros' ace and sleep guru. *New York Times*. Retrieved July 16, 2019, from https://www.nytimes.com/2019/07/09/sports/baseball/justin-verlander-all-star-sleep.html.

Chapter Two

The Parent as Curriculum Developer

HOW PARENTS CAN AUGMENT SCHOOLING BY TEACHING LESSONS THAT STRIVE FOR HAPPINESS

Schools cannot possibly teach everything a child needs for life; however, Nel Noddings (2009) argues persuasively that happiness should be part of the curriculum in schools. She writes,

> People want to be happy and, since this desire is well-nigh universal, we would expect to find happiness included as an aim of education. Its failure to appear among the aims usually stated might be a sign that Western society is still mired in a form of Puritanism, or, more generously, it may be generally believed that, as Orwell said, happiness cannot be achieved by aiming at it directly. If the latter is so, what should we aim at that might promote happiness? (p. 425)

Perhaps she is correct that teachers can promote happiness, but without heaping even more onto the backs of our educators, it is clear that parents certainly need to guide their children to develop lifelong skills to seek and nurture happiness. Of course, happiness is surely a personal construct, a mosaic of different things in different proportions that shift throughout the lifespan, or even from morning to night. It may be insipid to remark that happiness means different things to different people at different points in their lives; however, it seems evident that parents can do a great deal to set children up to strive for an authentic, meaningful understanding of personally relevant happiness.

To pull from Orwell's aforementioned claim, this chapter explores four practices that have significant bearing on striving for and managing happiness throughout the landscape of life. It is also vital to acknowledge the backchannel for this chapter, for it was the all-too-many tragic suicides of singer Amy Winehouse, skier Jeret Peterson, fashion designer Kate Spade, and actor Philip Seymour Hoffman that galvanized the impetus for these claims. Since one cannot buy happiness with money, fame, status, or achievement, what tenets should parents ensure that their children comprehend and practice when it comes to the development of "happiness"?

This chapter examines four recommendations for parents to embed in their parenting curriculum. The strategies highlight the areas of learning common to humanity but infrequently emphasized in typical curricular development: dealing with disappointment, picking yourself up when you are down, dealing with your demons, and pursuing patience. Taken together, the set honors the difficulties inherent in life regardless of career, family size, or geocultural context. As educator Sylvia Ashton-Warner (1963, p. 67) asks in her classic work *Teacher*, "Is there any time of life when tears and trouble are not a part of living?"

Dealing with Disappointment

Sorry, you won't win every game. You won't finish in the top three in every race, and you won't ace every exam or audition. Parents need to instill in their children the dignity and grace that comes with accepting outcomes, learning from mistakes, and dealing with disappointment. In 2019, the *New York Times* broke a devastating story about many famous parents who were guilty of bribing college admissions officers to induce acceptance of their children to elite colleges. Aside from the legal and ethical implications, the damage to the child's self-esteem is pernicious. The message to the child that they are not good enough on their own merit cuts deeply. Part of growing up is the learning that comes from falling and failing and coming up short.

Every child has procrastinated until the last minute to complete a report and received a less-than-satisfactory grade or not studied enough or properly for an important exam. Parents who do not let their children do their own work and make their own mistakes deprive their children of the important life lessons that come from these sorts of experiences. No one is good at everything, and sometimes we don't make wise decisions; yet, everyone needs to develop the presence of mind to handle disappointment. It is a vital part of life, and while no parent wants their child to experience multiple repeated pangs of disappointment, how else will the child develop mental and emotional fitness?

In her bestseller *Battle Hymn of the Tiger Mother* (2011), Amy Chua explains that the Chinese approach to parenting is "weakest when it comes to failure; it just doesn't tolerate that possibility" (p. 146). While the book is intensely provocative and inspirational, a world without failure seems unsustainable and seriously unsettling. Especially since the learning potential from missing the mark can be mined for its substantive load, it seems clear that while there are multiple considerations to keep in mind when guiding a child through deflating episodes, intolerance toward failure may be overly harsh.

When disappointment descends, and it will, the parent's job is to help the child understand that from this unfortunate situation, they can learn more about themselves and the world around them. Give them the opportunity to make sense of their choices and support them in understanding more about themselves, their relationships with others, and the implications of their actions or inactions. Do not immediately blame the system, the teacher, or the other party. Seek to help the child understand how point A leads to point B, identifying cause-and-effect relationships and response patterns so they can learn how their choices connect to outcomes. And even then, disappointment is a natural and normal part of life; even in our technological-whiz world, with keys and voice commands at our fingertips, breakdowns and glitches occur regularly. Your child needs to learn how to deal with disappointment, and it is your job to help.

Picking Yourself Up When You Are Down

The prevalence of opioid, vaping, alcohol, and substance abuse, as well as other addiction problems, in the United States today should cause parents alarm. No one wants their child to feel hurt, pain, or suffering. And there are clear cases where pharmaceutical drugs are medically indicated to alleviate human pain and suffering. *This section is not addressing such serious cases.* On a basic level, how does someone pick themselves up when they are feeling blue? Do we teach children to know themselves well enough to answer this question? What are socially and legally appropriate ways to decompress and relieve stress, disappointment, malaise, or loss that do not inflict bodily harm?

Children need to develop interests. They need to be exposed to the way music can reach into someone's soul and empathize with their experiences. They need to know that sitting or walking by water or through parks, nature trails, or forests can breathe hope and calm into dark times. If one is open to it, encounters with nature have the vital property to push a reset when the entire world seems off kilter. Exercise can take someone out of the moment and into immersive bodily kinesthetic experience far removed from destructive cyclical thoughts. There are choices a person has when they are feeling down. There are no quick fixes for painful relationship breakups, losing a job or loved one, or being humiliated publicly, but there are multiple ways people can help themselves heal, in addition to medication, therapy, and talking with friends or family.

Children need to develop a tool kit of activities that bring them toward happiness. Eating chocolate or other favored foods will never be enough to consistently pull everyone out of a funk, and eating disorders emergent from linking food to happiness are all too common. The categories of arts, sports/fitness, nature, crafts, and other interests can be central to the pursuit of happiness. Parents should notice children's interests and encourage interests for not only vocational or academic potential, but also their therapeutic capacity. Michael Steveni, writing in the late 1960s, was prescient: "Men of the future are, more than ever in the past, going to have to compensate to maintain their mental stability. They will have to be taught to find creative outlets, to make them for themselves" (1968, p. 232). Activities that move someone from destructive or depressive thought patterns to another zone of interest are vital to healthy healing practices. Parents can encourage and monitor the development of healthy pursuits. Simply, children need to be reminded that when they are feeling down, there are good choices they can make to help themselves feel better.

Dealing with Your Demons

> Education is to instruct the whole people in the proper care of the body, in order to augment the powers of that wonderful machine, and to prevent so much of disease, of suffering, and of premature death. The body is the mind's instrument; and the powers of the mind, like the skill of an artisan, may all be baffled, through the imperfection of their utensils. The happiness and the usefulness of thousands and tens of thousands of men and women have been destroyed, from not knowing a few of the simple laws of health. (Mann, 1867/1964, p. 95)

Education governs the care of physical, mental, social, emotional, and spiritual health. Even with professional assistance from doctors, teachers, therapists, and clergy, parents are on the front lines of the child's welfare. Moreover, it is clear from the first two recommendations that parents have a unique role in the monitoring and supervision of their child's mental and emotional health, nay the curricular development of the child's inner resources. The first principle addresses how to make cognitive sense of life's disappointments, and the second encourages the pursuit of healthy interests, asserting that varied activities promote reengagement in positive and generative aspects of living. Horace Mann, commissioner of education for the Commonwealth of Massachusetts in the late 19th century, implored his constituents as to the crucial role of education in stressing health.

> There is a higher art than the art of the physician; the art, not of *restoring*, but of *making* health. Health is a product. Health is a manufactured article, as much so as any fabric of the loom or the workshop, and, except in some few cases of hereditary taint, or of organic lesion from accident or violence, the how much, or the how little, health any man shall enjoy depends upon his treatment of himself, or rather, upon the treatment of those who manage his infancy and childhood, and create his habits for him. (Mann, 1867/1964, pp. 95–96)

Let it now be firmly stated that some people have very difficult family backgrounds and operate in contexts that are fractured, tense, loud, or oppositional to the individual's personality or dispositions. No one gets to choose their parents. This also means that we must live within a dynamic system and adapt to circumstances that no one else in the world fully understands no matter our communication skills or descriptive abilities.

All parents face their own demons and the consequences of their childhoods. "We've been so busy trying to rewrite our own pasts, we've blighted their present," says a character in *Harry Potter & the Cursed Child* (Rowling, Tiffany, & Thorne, 2016, p. 261). Reactive behavior from one's own autobiographical narrative is not a guarantee for parenting success. For example, if one was raised in an environment where emotions were bottled up and silenced, the next generation may elect to "let it all out," arguing loudly and frequently. The following generation may revert to the pattern of silence in reaction. And until the end of days, this unfortunate cycle perpetuates unless people face their foibles. Maria Montessori reminds us, "Until the adults consciously face their errors and correct them, they will find themselves in a forest of insoluble problems. And children, becoming in their turn adults, will be victims of the same error, which they will transmit from generation to generation" (1956/1970, p. 160).

Taming your demons means teaching children to identify their individual weaknesses, trigger points, and sensitivities as the parent faces down their own. Impulse control is one of the hardest skills to learn but essential to maintaining proper physical, emotional, mental, and social health. How does one stare down, walk away from, or put a lid on an escalating and destructive behavioral pattern? How does one stop smoking, gossiping, overeating, criticizing, or complaining? How does one apologize and start over after losing it in front of a child or with a child? How does one turn down an invitation to participate in something inappropriate?

The subtle inference here is moderately uncomfortable: The parent is the source text that the child learns from; ergo the parent is the curriculum. In concrete ways, the parent's display of prosocial behavior, modeling "please" and "thank you," holding the door open for others, and not grabbing food from buffet tables, teaches important behaviors for life. But that is the easy part. In truth, children recognize parental flaws more vividly than their parents ever will. Taming does not mean curing, it means managing through the demanding work of surveillance, vigilance, and self-control. As it says in *Ethics of the Fathers* (4:1), "Who is the strong? One who overpowers his inclination, as it is said . . . one who rules over one's spirit is better than one who conquers a city" (Proverbs 16:32). Children can be taught that everyone is flawed, but that means persistence and effort rather than submission and decline.

Pursuing Patience

Learning anything new takes time. Not everyone is blessed with both fine and gross motor skills. No one is born knowing how to ride a bike, flip an omelet, tie a shoe, clean a bathroom, whistle, drive a nail, or change a tire. In every field, from auto mechanics to aeronautics, "learning justifies learning" (Banner & Cannon, 1997, p. 15), because there is something purely amazing that happens as the learning process unfolds throughout time. "I could not do this before, but now I can," is the most motivating feeling in the world; however, in our era of shortcuts and quick fixes, it is tempting to give up and sell out rather than invest in something where the outcomes are uncertain and the trip is cumbersome. Finding patience means being patient with oneself, the subject at hand, and those helping you or whom you are trying to help. Deep learning requires even deeper pockets of patience.

During the last few years there has been ample discussion in the education world about the topic of grit. Angela Duckworth (2013, 2017) explains the construct as a representation of perseverance and passion for long-term goals, and a strong predictor of success. As a result of her notable research, the U.S. Department of Education has recommended that grit be taught in schools (Schechtman, DeBarger, Dornsife, Rosier, & Yarnall, 2013). Furthermore, Duckworth (2013) ends her inspirational TED talk with the following directive: "We need to be grittier about getting our kids grittier." Her articulate and impassioned plea honors the quest to improve the education for our nation's children. Credé (2018) critically reviews grit, clarifying and questioning some of Duckworth's claims and conclusions. Regardless of his critique, it may be worth adding that for grit to be secured as a habit of mind and practice, it best not be localized to academic subjects. Furthermore, what is the distinction between grit and patience?

Maxine Greene writes of what she calls a "wild patience." Pulling from a poem by Adrienne Rich called "Integrity," Greene seems to be referencing the line "a wild patience has taken me this far." At the end of her work *The Dialectic of Freedom* (1988), Greene leaves the reader with the following thought: "There is a need for a wild patience. And, when freedom is the question, it is always a time to begin" (p. 135). Greene's wild patience advances Duckworth's conceptualization of grit flush with stamina, drive, and intensity, adding notes of renewal, assurance, and society. She reminds us of our obligation to others in a democratic society, where individual achievement is situated within the context of communal responsibilities to others. Just like balance is a dynamic entity rather than a static posture, so to patience is active, or shall we say "wild."

Arts education scholar Elliot Eisner (2002) speaks of savoring an experience:

> Another lesson that the arts can teach education is the importance of taking one's time to relish the experience that one seeks. . . . If there is any lesson that the arts teach, it is the importance of paying close attention to what is at hand, of slowing down perception so that efficiency is put on a back burner and the quest for experience is made dominant. (p. 207)

Children need to be reminded that anything worth learning is worth learning well, and learning well means finding the patience to persist. Conceptually, to pay attention to details and attributes, to achieve lasting, sustainable growth, slow is good. People learn at different rates; be patient. People do not always do what you ask; be patient. Trying and trying again is frustrating; be patient. Parents need to be patient with their children, and children need to be patient with their parents; everyone needs to be patient with themselves. Let's encourage ourselves and our children to pursue patience.

CONCLUSION

Radio personality Dennis Prager often touts the catchphrase, "Happy people make the world better." Unfortunately, education for happiness is not a part of the curriculum conversation in American education today. In the grips of Common Core evidence-based learning accountability and assessment measures, understandings of curriculum in the United States today have been typically reduced to standards-based curriculum design with prescriptive instruction measured through high-stakes testing systems. The role of the parent as curriculum developer has never been more relevant or salient. Recess and the arts have been excised from many school programs to increase time for learning. Too often, increased learning only means more time on task test prep, learning and reviewing content to enhance test performance.

> If we allow our technologies to determine how we think about our intellectual processes, then one effect, which has been pervasive and very damaging to education, is to think of learning as a process analogous to recording symbols in the mind for later retrieval. The first thing we might note is that the human mind seems to be really quite inefficient at this kind of recording and faithful preservation throughout time. A sheet of paper or computer disk is much more reliable. Learning in this technology-analogous sense can be measured by how faithfully the records have been preserved when retrieved on a later test. This kind of testing goes on all the time in schools, and the results are taken very straightforwardly as evidence of learning (Egan, 1992, p. 49–50).

Evidence of learning for life requires broader framing than test performance can measure. It can be seen through the child's life and his/her choices. How does the child deal with disappointment when things don't go well or as expected? Does the child have healthy interests and activities? How does the child address their weaknesses and unhealthy patterns? Does the child exhibit patience with themselves, others, and learning? No one can guarantee anyone a lifetime of happiness, but given the trials and tribulations that we know will follow no matter the academic successes, should parents not devote ample time and energy to improving their child's chances for happiness? "Not everything can be said in a test score" (Eisner, 2017, p. 23). Parents can and should be the curriculum and the developer, learning with and for the child's (to quote Junie B. Jones) "bestest" chance at striving for happiness.

REFERENCES

Ashton-Warner, S. (1963). *Teacher*. New York: Touchstone Books.

Banner, J. M., & Cannon, H. C. (1997). *The elements of teaching*. New Haven, CT: Yale University Press.

Chua, A. (2011). *Battle hymn of the tiger mother*. New York: Penguin.

Credé, M. (2018). What shall we do about grit? A critical review of what we know and what we don't know. *Educational Researcher, 47*(9), 606–11.

Duckworth, A. L. (2013). *The key to success: Grit*. Retrieved July 16, 2019, from https://www.ted.com/talks/angela_lee_duckworth_the_key_to_success_grit?language_en#t-9644.

Duckworth, A. L. (2017). *Grit: Why passion and resilience are the secrets to success*. London: Vermilion.

Egan, K. (1992). *Imagination in teaching and learning: The middle school years*. Chicago: University of Chicago Press.

Eisner, E. (2002). *The arts and the creation of mind*. New Haven, CT: Yale University Press.

Eisner, E. (2017). *The enlightened eye: Qualitative inquiry and the enhancement of educational practice*. New York: Teachers College Press.

Greene, M. (1988). *The dialectic of freedom*. New York: Teachers College Press.

Mann, H. (1964). An educator speaks on education. In C. H. Gross & C. C. Chandler (Eds.), *The history of American education through readings* (pp. 94–101). Boston: D. C. Heath and Company. (Reprinted from Mann, *Lectures and Annual Reports on Education*, pp. 77–86, 144–46, 150–51, 1867, Cambridge.)

Medina, J., Benner, K., & Taylor, K. (2019, March 12). Actresses, business leaders, and other wealthy parents charged in U.S. college entry fraud. *New York Times*. Retrieved July 16, 2019, from https://www.nytimes.com/2019/03/12/us/college-admissions-cheating-scandal.html.

Montessori, M. (1956/1970). *The child in the family*. N. R. Cirillo, trans. New York: Avon. (Original work published 1956.)

Noddings, N. (2009). The aims of education. In D. Flinders & S. Thornton (Eds.), *The Curriculum Studies Reader*, 3rd ed. (pp. 425–38). New York: Routledge. (Reprinted from *Happiness and education*, pp. 74–93, by N. Noddings, 2003, Cambridge University Press.)

Rich, A. (1981). *A wild patience has taken me this far*. New York: W. W. Norton.

Rowling, J. K., Tiffany, J., & Thorne, J. (2016). *Harry Potter & the cursed child*, parts I and II. New York: Scholastic.

Schechtman, N., DeBarger, A. H., Dornsife, D., Rosier, S., & Yarnall, L. (2013). *Promoting grit, tenacity, and perseverance: Critical factors for success in the 21st century*. Washington, DC: U.S. Department of Education, Office of Education Technology. Retrieved July 16, 2019, from http://pgbovine.net/OET-Draft-Grit-Report-2-17-13.pdf.

Steveni, M. (1968). *Art and education*. New York: Atherton.

Chapter Three

Lessons from Mrs. Bird

A HUMOROUS LOOK AT HOW THE SEEMINGLY MINOR
"STUFF" OF DAILY LIFE IS EDUCATIONALLY RICH IN THE
DEVELOPMENT OF PERCEPTUAL ACUITY

"Mommy, why is she always sitting on her children?" asked Elisheva, age nine.

Mrs. Bird built a nest on my daughters' air conditioning unit in early May. When she first started bringing materials to the site, my daughters got nervous.

"Mommy, we tried to bang on the window, so that she could get the message to go build her nest somewhere else, but she just flies off and then returns with twigs and leaves when we are not looking."

In truth, the pile Mrs. Bird was building looked like a pathetic semblance of a nest—sort of squat and misshapen, not like those striking nests one saves as exemplars for school.

"Mommy, it is just like *The Best Nest*!" remarked Russy, age six.

She remembered P. D. Eastman's book where Mr. Bird tries unsuccessfully to locate a new home for his demanding wife, who desperately wants new digs. The "text-to-life" connection dazzled me. I had never heard this child make a connection between something she read and the life she lives. As an educational researcher and professor of teacher education, I was gripped by the obvious: Mrs. Bird is giving the lesson, and we are lucky she has chosen us to be in her classroom.

"Mommy, there are two eggs in the nest! I just saw them."

With excitement and joy, Elisheva and Russy called my attention to the small eggs in the misshapen nest on the air conditioning unit.

"Will they hatch? Will it hurt them if we turn on the air conditioner?"

"I really don't know . . ."

I sighed, feeling conflicted with the prospect of inadvertently harming our new neighbors. As it turned out, the early June heat wave didn't really give us another option for cooling off their room. But thank goodness it didn't harm the baby birds, because a half-week or so later, one of the eggs hatched.

"Mommy, Mrs. Bird is sitting on a grayish fluff ball. I think it is one of the birds!"

And so, it was. We waited for baby number two for several more days. And there it was—another grayish fluff ball.

"Why did this one hatch later, Mommy? Is this baby weaker?"

We watched Mrs. Bird sit on the baby birds, really perch right on top of the guys (or gals), in wonder and amazement. What dedication, what commitment this mother displayed. Even when my daughters tried to bang lightly on the window so she would move a bit and they could then get a peek at the babies, Mrs. Bird remained stalwart.

We marveled at their growth day by day. Baby bird number one grew huge, almost fully developed and mature. Mrs. Bird no longer sat on top of him/her, instead sitting to the side. Baby bird number two was still somewhat frail and rested under Mrs. Bird's protective body.

"When will they fly away? What happens if they can't fly? Who teaches them to fly?" The questions bombard our dinner table.

One day, Mr. Bird came to pay a visit.

"Mommy, Mr. Bird came, and Mrs. Bird flew off to get a break," said Rivka, age 11.

"So, where did she go, do you think?" I asked.

"She just needed to get away from the kids for a bit," said my daughter.

Hmm . . . like someone else we know?

And then there was the day Mrs. Bird flew off and just left the kids alone.

"They were squawking really loudly," said Rivka. "So, Mr. Bird came to babysit, and they just pecked at him. I think they were mad because he is not around enough."

Hmm . . .

Now we wait to see what happens next. Will Mrs. Bird push them off the nest? Will she just disappear and leave them to fend for themselves? Is there a message here for my own parenting and child-rearing?

And so, as the school year ends and all our wings are set to expand into the lushness and luxury of summer, with no homework, tests, quizzes, research papers, writing prompts, trifold displays, or book reports, we look at Mrs. Bird. Yes, she engaged the family with aesthetic and scientific inquiry. "Why such a squat-ish nest?" "Why does she sit on them?" Yes, she modeled habits of mind, including determination, commitment, professionalism, and a deep, enduring, profound sense of care for her youngsters. Okay, maybe she is just programmed to behave this way. Maybe she is just fulfilling her hard-wired destiny, but gosh, it sure is a phenomenal and beautifully demonstrated lesson in living life.

Oddly, a research study conducted in combination with the Lincoln Center Education Teacher Education Collaboration and the preservice teacher education program in the Stern College for Women at Yeshiva University, where I work, has a direct connection to the Mrs. Bird episode (Hirsch, 2012). One of the research findings concerns the relationship between control and authenticity. When the learning experience moved out of the college classroom to study public art (Dan Sinclair's *Fast Track and Speed Wheels*, 1990) in the NYC subway under Grand Central Station, the preservice candidates paid attention differently. "I have walked by this a million times, and I never noticed there was artwork here," was a frequent refrain. Furthermore, the shake-up from studying a work of art in a subway station, rather than in a museum or a traditional art venue, brought forth the sense that this was a purer learning experience, one that mimicked authentic, real-life learning. Clearly, this deliberately designed unit of study was not a spontaneous trip where passersby stopped and spotted something of interest. Yet, it delivered the same sense of "aha" as the moments in life when something arrests attention and brings the viewer to engage and notice deeply.

The parallel between Mrs. Bird on the air conditioner and Sinclair's work in the subway concerns access to the process of engagement. How do we guide children, adolescents, and adults of all ages to the real-world, firsthand, slow unfolding of seeing and seeing more that holds sway over imagination and inquiry? Like the classic optical illusion that flips the visual field (Is it an old lady or a young lady?), there is a thrill in seeing something one never before really properly noticed. And, close, patient, repeated noticing provides even more fine-grained detail and depth than binary illusions. The training of this perceptual acuity can be achieved in any field, in any season in life. Moreover, the potency of these moments lives in memory with powerful forward-leaning potential: "I will never look at a bird's nest the same way again."

As we think about the role of summer, with the glory of nature in full bloom and rapture, it seems that the world offers up a multitude of such authentic educational experiences. Yes, there is something terribly ironic about the sense that life starts when school stops, of which those of us who care about improving educational opportunity may certainly need to heed; however, it may also be important to consider the teachings from the world in which we live, the instruction parents have access to without funds from taxes or tuition. Parents can nurture their child's perception by authentically noticing and wondering aloud. They can answer their child's questions with their own questions or just leave the question be, for questions stand well on their own.

> Be patient toward all that is unsolved in your heart and try to love the questions themselves like locked rooms and books written in a very foreign tongue. Do not now seek the answers that cannot be given you because you would not be able to live them. And the point is, to live everything. Live the question now. Perhaps you will then gradually, without noticing it, live along some distant day into the answer. (Rilke, 1934/1993, p. 35)

Ah, Mrs. Bird, will you come back and teach us more?

REFERENCES

Hirsch, M. (2012). Co-constructing imaginative spaces: Public art in preservice teacher education. *Teaching Education, 23*(1), 9–24.

Rilke, R. M. (1934/1993). *Letters to a young poet.* H. Norton, trans. New York: W. W. Norton. (Original work published 1934.)

Sinclair, D. (1990). Fast track and speed wheels. Retrieved July 8, 2010, from https://www.nycsubway.org/perl/artwork_show?61.

Chapter Four

Contending with Sibling Rivalry

Inspiration from Jewish Texts

PERSPECTIVE FOR MINIMIZING AND MANAGING COMPETITION IN FAMILIES

Home is one of the most emotionally charged places in human consciousness. Like the classic Eagles song "Hotel California" ("You can check out any time you like, but you can never leave"), Citizen Kane's "Rosebud," or Harry Potter's scar, the wounds, dreams, and desires from our early years may follow us throughout our lives, sometimes deep, sometimes close to the surface, influencing who we become and the decisions we make. Typically, we don't get to select our children or parents, nor do we get to choose our siblings; however, we can choose how we relate to them and how we encourage our children to get along with one another.

So, let's begin by begging the question, have you ever experienced a feeling of sibling rivalry? That pang that your sibling received better treatment than yourself? If so, you are in good company, as there is a lot of sibling rivalry threaded throughout the Torah, the Jewish Bible. The purpose of this chapter is to examine sibling rivalry from a biblical perspective to determine if we can gain perspective to enhance how we guide brothers and sisters in relating to one another.

Many instances of sibling rivalry can be found in the Bible. These include events with Cain and Abel, Isaac and Ishmael, Jacob and Esau, Rachel and Leah, and Joseph and his brothers. Using a guided discovery model of learning, what are the essential characteristics or attributes of this set? What characteristics do these relationships have in common?

> There are siblings of the same genders pitted against one another.
>
> Individuals seem to be are vying for the same goal: the husband, the position of leadership, the blessing or birthright, acceptance, or a place of honor or distinction. And there is a sense of competition for one top prize.
>
> There are weighty implications. Cain wanders the world; if Leah had married Esau instead of Jacob perhaps the feud between the two dynasties would not have split the family into the seemingly irreparable conflict that exists even today.

With this background, let's go forward with three propositions.

> Proposition 1: The common theme of sibling rivalry in the Torah travels with our ancestors throughout the generations.
>
> Proposition 2: Sibling rivalry often occurs between siblings/people who seem to be similar in some way, vying for the same goal.
>
> Proposition 3: The situations are often complicated, emotionally challenging, and weighty; they matter deeply to those involved.

What insights from Jewish texts can guide our understanding of sibling rivalry in relating to our own siblings and family members?

First, let's define sibling rivalry. The individual's perception of sibling rivalry stems from the *perception of a competition*. There is a sense that there is something prized, desired by more than one person, so individuals perceive conflict relating to that item or status. They each feel pressure to achieve or possess it exclusively. With children, it could be a physical object (toy, phone, apartment, or money), emotional contact (hug, greeting, or text), or an experience (trip, concert, or restaurant meal).

> I can remember when I was engaged, I stepped right into it. My in-laws offered to pay for my flight to Chicago to spend the weekend with them, and I graciously accepted for a few days, until I found out that they didn't extend the same offer to my sister-in-law some years earlier, and this was causing stress in the family (as I heard from my husband, who heard from his brother, who heard from his wife), so I declined their offer and paid for the trip myself.

Everyone has their own stories of something being viewed as unfair by a sibling, a perceived inequity of experience. And the abundant and consequential outcome of such emotion, as seen in the Torah, suggests careful treatment of such emotions because of variegated perceptions and sensitivities.

Consider the following scenario: The first person to e-mail their story of sibling rivalry wins a $500 Amazon gift card. We have established competition, with one prize and one winner. Let's say a certain lady wins; other participants will no doubt feel envy and discontent. One can imagine people thinking something like, "She doesn't need it, I need it more," "She has so much, I really could have used it," "He cheated, he started before the clock," and so on.

This identifies two crucial concepts: perceived competition and jealousy. These are the building blocks of sibling rivalry, and understanding these components is essential in *managing* sibling rivalry. Note the deliberate word *manage* instead of *solving* sibling rivalry. Contemporary educational practice focuses on developing problem-solving skills, and while they are important, not all problems or challenging situations in life can be solved; some persist throughout our lives and, in fact, need to be managed. One doesn't solve the problem of making dinner nightly by making it once. It persists, like working, doing laundry, paying bills, and so forth. And, managing challenges in the relationship sphere is even harder than in the housework arena. Clearly, there are cyclical patterns of time when things are going well and going less well, and one has to make adjustments. One can make the case that the wealth of examples of sibling rivalry throughout the Bible communicates the message that sibling rivalry is a situation to be managed throughout a lifetime.

Next, let us unpack the two building blocks, perceived competition and jealousy. First, perceived competition can be framed from a Talmudic perspective (the Talmud is the Jewish book of law). The Talmud (Shabbos: 10b) warns parents not to show favoritism between their children: "A person must never distinguish one of his sons from the others, for a weight of two *selaim* of fabric which Jacob gave Joseph more than his other sons (in the form of a striped coat) made his brothers envious of him, and the affair led from one thing to another until our forefathers ended up descending to Egypt." This passage highlights the need to be mindful that parental actions can foment jealousy. Proverbs (14:30) is quite graphic: "Envy rots the bones." Envy destroys people. Envy destroys families, relationships. It is that terrifyingly potent.

I was a pretty shy kid, pretty hard on myself, and my father, z"tl (*zecher tzaddik l'vracha*, may his memory be a blessing), wanted to pick up my spirits so he made me this gorgeous collage of inspirational quotes and images; he worked on it without my knowing for a very long time in the basement and it was incredible. I still remember the orange background of the poster board. He hung it in my room as a surprise. But my siblings were livid and hated me for it. Ultimately, I had to get rid of it, and that cleared up the animosity. I wonder if they even remember it today, and G-d forbid, I would not ever bring it up. It was awful.

Now, it is equally fascinating that we also find in Proverbs (15:30), precisely one chapter later, "Good tidings fatten bones." The expansion that occurs when one hears good news can be further contextualized by the phrase that precedes this particular sentence. The complete sentence reads, "Enlightened eyes gladden the heart, good tidings fatten bones." Perhaps we can further suggest that "enlightened eyes" refers to perspective and how opening our eyes can help us understand that the notion of perceived competition is truly illusory in deception.

"Enlightened eyes" suggests that what matters is how one interprets or makes sense of situations, the perspective one has of the event. It seems that fundamental to managing sibling rivalry, while envy may originate as visceral emotion, is the calibration of one's orientation. One has the choice to view something as competition or approach such situations with an alternative mindset. Such understanding can be developed from a religious perspective or a special education perspective. The religious perspective asserts that, "G-d gives a person everything he deserves and everything he needs. Anything a person does not have is therefore something which he either does not deserve or does not need" (Brisk, 1993, p. 137). Similarly, Richard Lavoie, a prominent special educator and motivational speaker, clarifies this point in his distinction between the words *fair* and *equal*. In his famous "F.A.T. City" video, Lavoie (as cited in Rosen & Lavoie, 2004) explains that giving children what they need is fair. If one child needs more time to answer a question, then do not rush him/her just because other children accomplish the task more quickly. If a child needs the teacher to both say and write directions, then it is not an issue of equality if all the children do not receive this differentiation. Lavoie explains the similar message often told to preservice teacher education candidates: "The whole class does not need to get a band-aid if one child has skinned her knee." But when it comes to sibling rivalry, children have tremendous difficulty and emotional fervor over such perceived inequities. Why?

We raise children to function as both individuals and members of a collective unit without identifying clear protocols for when to assume each role. The Jewish text *Ethics of Our Fathers* sums this up in the following aphorism: "If I am not for myself, then who will be for me; But, if I am only for myself, what am I?" The conflict expressed herein has no neat solution that operates with fixed periodicity. Case by case, moment by moment, moral individuals must weigh options, deliberate alternatives, and imagine outcomes in advance of action. The competing memberships build tension and dissent, with accompanying cries of injustice and inequity: "But that is not fair," "You did not do that for me," "She/he always gets more!"

This brings us to a powerful claim. Point two: We may seem similar on the surface, but each of us is destined for a different outcome. There is no perceived competition. It is an illusory mirage. It is our job as parents to help our children recognize what is special about them, what aptitudes and capacities they possess, and what areas need more attention and development but not in a way that diminishes other family members. There is no perceived competition. It is not I have and therefore you have not. We have been given different gifts. "After all, no two people are alike, and everyone must have something in excess of another" (Brisk, 1993, p. 136). "She is taller," "He is smarter," "They are more fortunate." The notion of life as a perceived competition needs to fall away. And if so, we dismantle jealousy as well.

Indeed, the Torah offers us a model emblematic of a supportive sibling relationship through what could have been a competitive and fractious exchange. The relationship between Moses and Aaron offers a good paradigm for understanding both the tension and resolution of sibling rivalry. Aaron was the elder brother, and Moses was the younger sibling; however, Moses was appointed by G-d to be the Leader of Israel. And, even though he was the younger brother, his older brother Aaron was happy for him, without a shred of jealousy. As it says in Exodus (4:14), when G-d tells Moses that Aaron is "going out to meet you and when he sees you, he will rejoice in his heart."

The Talmud, in Shabbos 139a, expands on this sentiment to tell us that because of this expression of pure happiness for his brother, Moses, Aaron was awarded his status as the head priest. Precisely because of his rejoicing about the accomplishments of his sibling, he is awarded his position. The Jewish principle of *Middah K'Neged Middah*, measure for measure, applies here: Aaron is happy in his heart for his brother Moses, so G-d rewards him with the position of high priest, who wears a special breastplate, the *Choshen Mishpat*, over his heart.

The Talmud also tells us the backstory that, in fact, Moses lost the position of high priest. He was initially supposed to also hold this position (Zevachim 20) but was removed because he told G-d to "please send someone else" to take the Jewish people out of Egypt (Exodus 4:13). Because he tried to get out of his leadership role, G-d removed this portion of his leadership and reassigned it to Aaron.

Aaron was subsequently responsible for overseeing the infamous golden calf episode. As a punishment, G-d wanted to strip Aaron of the position of high priest and transfer it back to Moses. The Midrash says that Moses prayed on behalf of Aaron that he should keep the position. To review, Moses was supposed to assume the role of high priest, but G-d took it away. Now he has the chance to have it restored to him but instead prays that his brother should have the honor, and G-d listens to his request. We see through this episode the selfless outlook the brothers had for one another. The Bible offers this example of sibling relationships at the highest level, one that respects individuality with its ensuing unique talents and different blessings. The relationship between Moses and Aaron also lucidly showcases supportive sibling responses.

In summary:

Sibling rivalry exists in the world.
We can manage it by managing our outlook and behavior.

Next, the pragmatics: How do we mobilize this mindset in our own lives and develop this perspective with our children? In their classic manual on sibling rivalry, *Siblings Without Rivalry* (1987), Adele Faber and Elaine Mazlish poignantly dedicate the work, "To all the grown-up siblings who still have a hurt child inside them." It is no surprise that sibling rivalry can become a persistent cross-generational problem if left unaddressed. Sibling rivalry can wound children, and when these children grow to be wounded adults, they may perpetuate perspectives of rivalry and competition in their own parenting and family relationships. The pain, anguish, and rupture within and across families leaves lasting damage. Fortunately, the Bible offers practical wisdom that can be useful in our own lives, specifically suggesting three practical guidelines to minimize and manage sibling rivalry.

First, as we have already alluded, we must encourage our children to answer the aptitude and interest questions: What are they good at? What do they enjoy doing? What are their natural gifts? While recognizing that some capacities and interests only unfold throughout time through experiences later in life, it is important to continually encourage self-reflection with such questions. Stoke the quest for self-knowledge and mindful reflection to enable children to understand, acknowledge, seek, and build strength upon strength, while always stressing that humility grounds aptitude authentically. One turn of phrase borrowed from the current teacher education certification exam, known as the edTPA, relates to personal assets. So, encourage children to consider their personal assets and how personal assets or talents can shape appropriate, positive, meaningful, and satisfying contributions today and in the years to come. How can we help ourselves, others, and the larger communities of which we are a part?

Second, this brings us to capital "We." All of us are children of G-d, and so the potential for sibling rivalry beyond familial lines certainly exists. We are in this one larger family unit, humankind, which means that the work parents do in their own families to develop and guide children individually must be contextualized by the orientation to membership in society. The relationship work in the service of raising young in family units develops social skills in relation to the rest of humanity. This is part of parental responsibility. Clearly, how one relates to his or her siblings teaches the child about the skill set for relating to others, the rest of humanity, the rest of the "family." Each parent has an obligation to pay attention to how she/he models relationships with siblings. Our children are always watching us.

Lastly, family units are the proving grounds for understanding group dynamics and more macro civic bonds. We need to teach children that family membership has its own set of expectations and responsibilities. Remind them that they do not inhabit this world alone, they are enmeshed in a network, part of a larger whole. Two concerns present simultaneously: What does it mean to pursue your own talents and G-d-given gifts within the frame of community? How do we behave not only toward our family members, but also as a family? Do we provide opportunities that demonstrate the family unit acting as a collectively integrated and unified entity?

Obviously, it is essential that adults cultivate individual one-on-one relations with each child, and this exclusive parent–child time is invaluable. But figuring out how to act as a unit when there are multiple quirky members is another skill set that develops understanding of group dynamics, selflessness, and empathy. Collectively shared experiences generate history and legacy. And so as parents we also need to develop the notion of us, we, our family.

A short anecdote: I was shopping with some of my children and one of my daughters said to another, "What are you doing with that dress? We are Hirsches; we don't wear yellow." It is, in fact, a family joke that we don't look good in yellow-hued clothing. But the implication recognizes shared knowledge, humor, ritual, celebration, and all the proverbial stuff that is done as a family. The moments of shared memories matter a great deal, and the skills required to work synergistically in a group structure are also vital. The community development piece is a parent's job as well and can be modeled and understood through the expectations and responsibilities of family membership. The sense of one's self as an individual and as a member of the family unit is crucial. This perspective can model insight that orients children to external human relationships; as Jewish teaching asserts, all people were created *B'Tzelem Elokim*, in the image of G-d.

Contending with sibling rivalry can reduce perceived competition and jealousy, which threatens dialogue, collaboration, and community. Is this too pie in the sky that the treatment between brothers and sisters illuminates best practices and skills for working together, understanding multiple perspectives, and situating individuality in the larger frame of humanity? "Raising up decent and principled children has been the desire of humankind for millennia" (Sizer and Sizer, 1999, p. xiii). So, while sibling rivalry will continue to rear its ugly head, defense against these "dark arts" can be managed with intentionality and insight.

REFERENCES

Brisk, H. (1993). *Torah concepts for teachers and parents: Educating our children*. Spring Valley, NY: Feldheim.

Faber, A., & Mazlish, E. (1987). *Siblings without rivalry: How to help your children live together so you can live too*. New York: Avon.

Rosen, P., & Lavoie, R. D. (2004). *How difficult can this be? Understanding learning disabilities: Frustration, anxiety, tension, the F.A.T. city workshop* [Film, educational DVD]. Alexandria, VA: Eagle Hill Foundation.

Sizer, T. R., and Sizer, N. F. (1999). *The students are watching: Schools and the moral contract*. Boston: Beacon.

Chapter Five

"Reading" Schools

A Primer

CRITICAL NOTES AND INQUIRY FOR MAKING SCHOOLING DECISIONS WITH MINDFULNESS AND INTENTION

How do parents decide which school to send their children to? This dilemma can be challenging each time parents make a school selection, and it can be difficult no matter how many previous times this decision is faced. From early childhood settings to high school, we weigh neighbors' opinions, take expert counsel, speak with former educators, receive advice from Realtors, and hopefully listen to our children. But really, how can one ever really know that they are making the absolute correct choice for their child? In fact, no human can ever be entirely certain of this answer, but there are ways to make sense of schools; there are objective and intuitive factors that parents can pick up on if they can learn to "read schools."

The notion of "reading schools" stems in part from the work of Rosario and Collazo (1981), who acknowledge the role of aesthetic codes in school contexts and the way these features formally and informally influence teaching and learning. This orientation suggests that like a book with text written on the page that is accessible if you understand the language of the text, school organizations offer clues, codes, and messages about the culture, climate, curriculum, and community of the school that one can make sense of if the language of the school discourse is understood.

Elliot Eisner's (2002) three-part definition of curriculum (implicit, explicit, and null curriculum) offers an additional frame to see beyond the typical set of assumptions parents make about schools. Eisner delineates the following categories:

Explicit curriculum: This is the official school curriculum as promulgated on the curriculum frameworks, websites, and formal school documentation, including lesson plans, homework assignments, and conversations with school personnel. Of course, this is the intended education, the education that is planned for the child, not what may actually happen in reality. For example, the students were supposed to "cover" chapters 1–8 in the mathematics text but ran out of time and only addressed the first six.

Implicit curriculum: This is the hidden curriculum that emerges from the covert messages, aesthetic codes, social norms, and general classroom or school ambience. For example, do all teachers have bulletin board space? Are the messages posted at the school office outdated? Do faculty have to follow the same dress code as the student body? The implicit curriculum pays attention to the nuances that may undergird such observations.

Null curriculum: This refers to what is not taught, what is absent from the school program, "what the students never have the opportunity to learn" (Eisner, 2002, p. 159). For example, does the school offer art, music, coding, or gym? Do the students learn about Thanksgiving, Juneteenth, or Veterans Day? Students learn that what is omitted is not of value or significance to the adult decision makers.

This chapter offers the reader a set of guidelines to begin to "read schools." As an individual who has spent a lot of time in schools in various capacities, as an educational researcher, teacher educator, assistant principal, classroom teacher, specialty arts teacher, library assistant, assistant teacher, and substitute teacher, the multiple roles evince strong intuition that the school walls, and not only the people inhabiting the school community, speak. In addition, since parents spend their hard-earned money to provide children with a balanced and rigorous education, it is crucial to have a heuristic mechanism to augment the school decision-making process; however, before introducing a set of domains to advance thinking about school organizations, four notes of caution:

Autobiography is a biased estimator. As discussed in the first chapter, "The Mathematics of Mothering," you are not the same as your child and your child is not you. Just because some school type or teacher's style did not work for you, remember that is not enough of a reason to entirely dismiss the school or this type of teacher for your child. Be wary of allowing your own bad or good experiences to influence your reading of schools.

Beware of bells and whistles. Noted anthropologist Franz Boas tells the story of taking a Kwakiutl leader from the Pacific Northwest on a visit to New York City in the early 20th century. Boas reports that the leader was most interested in the brass balls on the hotel banisters and the bearded ladies exhibited in Times Square (Morgan, 1997). With respect to schools, having the most up-to-date technological resources may be impressive, but knowing how and when to use them effectively to enhance and advance learning is much more so. "Attention may be captured by the hoopla and ritual that decorate the surface of organizational life rather than by the deeper and more fundamental structures that sustain these visible aspects" (Morgan, p. 152).

You are not awarding blue ribbons. The U.S. Department of Education's "Blue Ribbon Schools Program" recognizes schools serving disadvantaged students that demonstrate dramatic growth in academic performance or any public or private school that performs in the top 10% on the state assessments (https://www2.ed.gov/programs/nclbbrs/index.html). When you are selecting a school for your child, you are not trying to find the best school in the area, you are trying to find the best school for your child, and these objectives may not always be synonymous. One morning on New Jersey Transit, a lady was actually yelling at a gentleman standing near her on the train, "I am not saying it is not a good school, I am just saying it wasn't right for my child!"

Stop feeling threatened. When parents of similarly aged children make different school selections, oftentimes one of the sets of parents feels threatened by or uncomfortable with the fact that the other family has rendered a different decision. It is as if because someone else has selected another path for their child, it somehow casts a shadow on their own decision-making, sowing seeds of doubt in kind. If one has been careful in making the school decision, they should breathe deeply and feel confident that all the leg work has been done appropriately for their child at this point in time.

The next section introduces a guideline for reading schools so that when it is time to make a decision about schools, parents can be informed with a set of criteria to help make sense of the open houses, school tours, and backyard discussions. It should help maximize time and energy in making this important selection.

WHAT ARE WE "READING"?

The features of school organizations can be thought of in terms of physical resources, human resources, and curricular resources. The following list of questions and directives about school resources is not exhaustive nor is it applicable to every school setting, but it should give parents a sample of the types of things to observe, question, and be curious about.

Physical Resources

Brand new buildings, converted trailers, or traditional public-school facilities nuance the atmosphere of educational practice. The features of the physical environment yield specific energy and particular shape to the learning that happens in the space.

What does the exterior of the building look like?
Is there ample parking for faculty and visitors?
How does the building accommodate physical challenges?
Does the yard look clean or are there food wrappers lying about?
Is the outdoor play area nice?
Are the entrances secured?
What do the teachers' rooms look like and sound like?
Are fire and emergency procedures neatly and prominently posted?
Does every student have a desk?
Are the desks arranged in the same configuration in every room?
Where is technology used? Is there a science lab? A library? A gym?
Are the walls decorated appropriately? Is there evidence of children's work? Does all the children's work look exactly the same?
How are the hallways used? What sounds do you hear as you tour the school?

Human Resources

Teachers are the keys to school improvement (Sergiovanni, 2000). Educational leaders steer the ship, but teachers are directly responsible for the educational progress of children. And anyone in schools who children encounter, including secretaries, bus drivers, janitors, the school nurse, and the librarian, have the potential to impact their lives in profound ways.

How are new teachers mentored?

What is the teacher turnover rate?

What is the professional background of the staff?

What is the role of assistant teachers?

Do teachers have the opportunity to work collaboratively?

What kind of accreditation do the teachers hold?

What type of support staff exists for children with special needs? Gifted education?

What kind of interaction does the principal have with the students? When does this happen?

What are the home-school communication practices?

Does the school provide professional development for its faculty?

How does the office staff answer the phones? (Call and see.)

How responsive are teachers and principals to e-mail?

What is the nature of the interaction between teachers?

What is the educational philosophy of the teacher?

How is the school involved with its surrounding community?

How do people in the school talk to one another? To the children?

How does the leader spend most of his/her day?

How does the secretary talk to the leader? And vice versa?

Curricular Resources

"The curriculum is a mind-altering device" (Eisner, 2002, p. 148). The nutrient matter of the curriculum, explicit, implicit, and null, coupled with the professional pedagogic practices of the instructors, signal educational progress, stasis, or decline. Furthermore, attention to the facets of classroom management, discipline policies, and educational philosophy significantly contour the teaching and learning approaches that ultimately shape educational outcomes.

What are the classroom materials like?

Does the school promote prizes, rewards, and contests?

Is there a unified discipline policy across all grades? Where is this documented?

What can you learn from the school website? What is missing that you might expect to see there?

What is the orientation to curricular instruction: behavioral, constructivist, traditional, discipline based, or experiential (Posner, 2004)?

Are there opportunities for interactive collaborative learning experiences both in and out of the classroom?

What is the stated purpose of homework?

Where does character education fit in?

Are subject-specific skills (i.e., scientific method, writing process) taught?

What are some of the special school events or rituals?

What kinds of field trips does the school typically plan?

What role do the state standards play?

What happens when a child misbehaves?

How much time is spent on each subject daily, weekly, and monthly?

Are grading policies transparent?

Do teachers use assessment measures other than quizzes or tests?

What about community service hours?

There are differences between schools. The differences may or may not matter for your child and his/her educational needs. I know that every parent wants to select the right school for their child. Knowing more about what to look for, listen for, and question may assist with this weighty decision–making process. Please note that the checklists are not exhaustive nor predictive. Furthermore, the meaning of the presence or absence of each item individually or collectively does not clearly augur in one direction or another. Each parent is astute enough to draw their own set of conclusions and interpretations for their child with his/her particular concerns. The goal of this chapter is to provide a guide for noticing what there is to be noticed (Greene, 2001) in the search to make sense of school organizations. The bottom line is to trust your instinct, but what is instinct exactly? According to Regan and Brooks (1995, p. 33), "It is a natural mental ability, strongly associated with experience." The intent is that this introduction to reading schools will assist parents in experiencing schools with greater scope, clarity, and insight, and inform a difficult decision-making process with more attention to the crucial aspects of educational organizations.

REFERENCES

Eisner, E. (2002). *The arts and the creation of mind.* New Haven, CT: Yale University Press.

Greene, M. (2001). *Variations on a blue guitar: The Lincoln Center Institute lectures on aesthetic education.* New York: Teachers College Press.

Morgan, G. (1997). *Images of organization.* Thousand Oaks, CA: Sage.

Posner, G. (2004). *Analyzing the curriculum,* 3rd ed. New York: McGraw-Hill.

Regan, H., & Brooks G. (1995). *Out of women's experience: Creating relational leadership.* Thousand Oaks, CA: Corwin.

Rosario, J., & Collazo, E. (1981). Aesthetic codes in contest: An exploration in two preschool classrooms. *Journal of Aesthetic Education, 15*(1), 71–82.

Sergiovanni, T. (2000). *The lifeworld of leadership: Creating culture, community, and personal meaning in our schools.* San Francisco, CA: Jossey-Bass.

U.S. Department of Education. National Blue Ribbon Schools Program. *U.S. Department of Education.* Retrieved November 12, 2009, from https://www2.ed.gov/programs/nclbbrs/index.html.

Part II

For Teachers (and Parents)

Chapter Six

Reclaiming the Art of Listening

WHY LISTENING SHOULD MATTER MORE IN TODAY'S EXCEEDINGLY DOMINANT VISUAL CULTURE

Class, with your reading buddies, please return to your seats and locate three passages of descriptive writing in the novel. Mark your selections with Post-its and record the page numbers and descriptive language in your reading journals. Who can repeat the instructions? Good. Who can summarize the directions in your own words? Excellent.

Economizing every moment in the classroom requires that the teacher truncate directions and clarify instructions with exactitude. Students need to know precisely what to do and how to do it efficiently. The educational stakes are high, and each moment of every task matters. There can be no lapse in the choreography of the classroom as students travel from rug area to buddy spots and back. Yet, what are the unintended consequences of repeating directions and summarizing instructions ad nauseam? If one knows that someone is going to repeat the instructions and review the directions again, why bother listening the first time? And is listening only a form of verbal mirroring? This chapter explores three facets of listening that are becoming educationally endangered: listening to self, listening to others, and listening to the world.

LISTENING TO SELF

My student teachers often have the darndest time selecting a research question of their own choice. They are asked, "What are you interested in knowing more about?" "What are you curious about?" They avoid introspection and the deep knowing that comes from reflective inquiry like the plague, pleading, "Tell me what you think I should research." It is curious as to why it is so hard for some to sit quietly with their own thoughts: What happened to the ability to harness the mind and probe possibilities, imagine outcomes, and weigh alternatives? To be mundane, there are aspects of listening to self that are significantly more complicated than selecting a research paper topic. How can we expect young people to proudly choose an occupation that draws on their talents and interests if they have never been given an opportunity or the tools to seek them from within?

Moreover, children and adults of all ages must reckon with tough moral choices throughout their lives. The peer pressure faced by students in today's schools permeates both real-life and virtual spaces. How should a student respond when they receive a forwarded e-mail viciously mocking a fellow classmate? When an older sibling has a copy of last year's science final, can the current student study from this exam if the teacher is known to use the same exam year after year? If a teen is at a party with drugs but doesn't use them personally, what is the best course of action? The development of character and moral fiber requires the generation of an inner voice to provide direction and counsel in times of uncertainty. Students need to learn how to listen to themselves.

Many student teachers argue that guilt has no place in education. They retort that it can cause psychological damage if a child feels bad about himself/herself. On the contrary, they are asked, "Haven't you ever done anything wrong and then felt so awful about it that you told yourself that you would never do that thing again?" Perhaps, it is the word *guilt* that rubs them the wrong way. If we had a word in our language for listening to self, then perforce they would understand the potential for redirection and change sparked by the dulcet tones of conscience within each of us.

LISTENING TO OTHERS

Many people think that listening to others only involves relating the experiences of others to their own lives. It is continually perplexing to experience conversations with people who listen to parallel how they have had a similar experience, or also lost a loved one, or even had a more severe illness than the one just described. When did listening become a corollary to social besting? Yes, text-to-self connections and other critical thinking skills, for example, perspective taking and adopting different frames of knowing, involve drawing relationships between the self and others. That is all well and good, but can our students develop an ethic of care that doesn't repeatedly insert their own set of experiences and emotions in the way of someone else's?

Philosopher Iris Marion Young (1997) argues for "asymmetrical reciprocity" in seeking to understand one another: "If I assume that there are aspects of where the other person is coming from that I do not understand, I will be more likely to be open to listening to the specific expression of their experience, interests, and claims. Indeed, one might say that this is what listening to a person means" (p. 49). Because no one can really walk a mile in someone else's moccasins, what can be done is to walk alongside and listen closely to the cadence of their footsteps. As students are taught history or literature, they can be reminded that as much as people can understand another person's perspective, there is much that cannot truly be understood. Moreover, the desire to reduce another person's set of experiences into a neat, tidy package disrespects the uniqueness and particularity of human life.

In addition, teachers have long attended to qualitative aspects of their student's voices to distinguish motivation, distress, or confusion. Subtle changes in volume, pitch, rhythm, tone, or pace may indicate the need for further attention. The hesitation in a child's voice may signify that the conversation has entered sensitive territory and the student would rather not respond at the moment. Teachers can likewise instruct their students in the acquisition of these receptive skills—so important to interpersonal communication, the development of sensitive and respectful relationships, and good parenting practices.

Noddings (2009) imagines a missing dimension in education in a humorous but woefully ironic dialogue between a visitor from another world and a representative educator, Ed. The visitor comments, "It struck me as odd that, although your people spend much of their time in homemaking, parenting, and recreation, these topics are rarely addressed in your schools" (p. 436). Ed dismisses the visitor's comments with refutations about full schedules and the improper intrusion of these topics into school life. The visitor later continues, "It has to do with happiness." Listening to others is part and parcel of the fabric of good relationships, and children need to know that happiness is not about material acquisition (as outlined with greater depth in chapter 2), but the deep satisfaction that comes from communing with someone for whom you care deeply.

LISTENING TO THE WORLD

The visual components of classrooms have overtaken the audio by leaps and bounds. Teachers and students can create magical displays of sight and sound with futuristic appeal; perambulating images bounce, twirl, and pulse from even the most sanitized internet sites. A colleague of mine who supervises student teachers was mesmerized by a Smart Board presentation in which the students virtually observed objects floating or sinking in water on the screen. My response to him was less enthusiastic: "Why don't the second graders just experiment with real water in the classroom? Why learn about water virtually? Don't children need to touch, feel, and observe with firsthand, real-world experiences?"

Moreover, while the proliferation of AirPods, earbuds, and Bluetooth technology is clearly aural, the digitized nature of such mechanisms simultaneously requires shrinking away from the world, ignoring the physical and social environment in favor of a more introverted focus. Yes, close listening is good. We want students to connect with music and also call their parents occasionally; however, when we have not taught our children to appreciate the small sounds of morning, the thud of the newspaper outside the door, or the birds chirping in springtime, we have lost something very special, a valuable aural capacity. Even Jaron Lanier, father of virtual reality, frequently bemoans the digitization of sound, loss of musical complexity, and absence of generationally stylized music in the technological soundscape of the internet. He believes that the internet "for all its convenience, its ubiquity, its success, is flattening our culture" (Horne, 2010).

During his life, my father never forgot the sound of rain on the tin roof of his childhood home in Western Pennsylvania. In his memoirs just prior to his death, he penned, "And always, always, I will hear the threatening drum-like rumble of rain on the tin roof of our little wooden house/I've known from childhood hours/The modulated din/Of things and thundershowers/Upon a roof of tin" (Ungar, 2001, n.p.).

It was a proud day for me when one of my daughters remarked how she thought the "bump-bump" sound her wheelie backpack made as she dragged it down a jagged sidewalk was "cool." Unnatural quiet or odd sounds are also vital portents of danger. "When you see something, say something" is really only partially correct; listening may also play a powerful role in alerting others of a potential problem. The sounds of silence, which include Simon & Garfunkel's lyrics, the real, thick silence of night, and the silence of the resistant student under the hoodie in the corner, are all worth our attention.

CONCLUSION

Parents used to ask their children, "Did you listen to the teacher?" or "Are you listening to me?" Today, listening has achieved a national focus as a coveted member of the Common Core Standards (2010). The publicly available document identifies "speaking and listening" as a core domain of the English Language Standards for all grades K–12. Within each grade level, "speaking and listening" is further delineated into two large categories, comprehension and collaboration, and the presentation of knowledge and ideas (www.corestandards.org). The skills described in the document, for example, "working with peers to promote civil, democratic discussions and decision-making" from the grades 11–12 frame or "create audio recordings of stories or poems" from the grade 2 band, are valuable standards of achievement that teachers and parents can use to ascertain progress. But let us not forget there are crucial facets of listening unconnected with speaking or following directions: listening to yourself, listening to others, and listening to the world around us. As Sylvia Ashton-Warner (1963, p. 214) reminds, "I always find . . . that if I keep quiet I learn something."

REFERENCES

Ashton-Warner, S. (1963). *Teacher*. New York: Simon & Schuster.

Horne, E. (2010, January 4). Jaron Lanier wonders about new music, the internet, and octopuses with Robert Krulwich. *wnycstudios.org*. Retrieved July 16, 2019, from https://www.wnycstudios.org/podcasts/radiolab/articles/91936-jaron-lanier-wonders-about-new-music-the-internet-and-octopusses-with-robert.

National Governors Association Center for Best Practices and the Council of Chief State School Officers. (2010). Common Core Standards Initiative. *Corestandards.org*. Retrieved July 16, 2019, from http://www.corestandards.org/.

Noddings, N. (2009). The aims of education. In D. Flinders & S. J. Thornton (Eds.), *The curriculum studies reader*, 3rd ed. (pp. 425–37). New York: Routledge. (Reprinted from *Happiness and Education*, pp 74–93, by N. Noddings, 2003, Cambridge University Press.)

Ungar, J. I. (2001). *Memoirs*. Unpublished manuscript.

Young, I. M. (1997). *Intersecting voices: Dilemmas of gender, political philosophy, and policy.* Princeton, NJ: Princeton University Press.

Chapter Seven

Out of the Box and Between the Lines

ENCOURAGING CHILDREN TO BALANCE CREATIVITY AND RESPONSIBILITY

> Teacher: Sandy, your book report is missing several key components. You've neglected to include the author's last name, the setting, the plot summary, and new vocabulary words.
> Sandy: Yes, I took a risk. You always tell us to be creative!

Oftentimes creativity gets a bum rap as an excuse for not following directions or paying close attention. Sometimes the term "creative" is synonymous with "off task," just as "shows leadership potential" frequently replaces descriptors of "bossiness." There is a clear need to recompose creativity within 21st-century educational nomenclature. How can teachers promote creativity among their students in this age of accountability, assessment, standards, and benchmarks? And how can teachers leverage these competing tensions in their own professional practice?

This chapter explores five spiraling considerations to reframe creativity in the classroom. They are not intended as universal principles, but rather grid marks to position creativity within the discourse of instructional design, implementation, and assessment.

1. Creativity does not mean "anything goes."
2. Creativity is born from time, patience, and dedication, which are often invisible.
3. Creative expression is not hard to evaluate.

4. Creativity requires persistence, resilience, and increased comfort with failure.
5. Creativity crosses all disciplines, including pedagogy.

CREATIVITY DOES NOT MEAN "ANYTHING GOES"

A scholarship opportunity was lost by this author because of a quarter-centimeter. The directions clearly stipulated that the essay text had to be between the designated margins of one inch on each side of the application. In truth, my father was very ill, and there was no time, energy, or motivation to fix the error. This resulted in the submission of a tear-stained, asymmetrically centered essay that no jury ever read. Nonetheless, an important lesson was firmly established that day about the marriage of content and format, ensuring that directions are reread over and over again to double check for accuracy and detail.

Adherence to procedure is not a vehicle for organizational evil. Yes, bureaucracy can frustrate with its minutia of specifications. However, it is not a bad lesson to learn that one has to play by the rules. My husband tells the story of a Little League game in Peoria, Illinois, where he hit a home run and, rounding third, removed his helmet before home plate. "You're out!" called the umpire. In life, following the rules matters.

CREATIVITY IS BORN FROM TIME, PATIENCE, AND DEDICATION, WHICH ARE OFTEN INVISIBLE

Some semesters ago a preservice student wanted to create a curriculum unit for her arts in education course on the topic of plating desserts. It was an atypical choice for a discipline-based arts education class that focuses on music, drama, dance, and visual arts. The essential question guiding the assignment asked, "What are the key arts concepts or skills that your students will learn through this unit?" At first, she didn't know. After researching the topic, she settled on the concepts of color, contrast, line, and shape. The unit began with sauces and plate shapes, and culminated in an end-of-the-year party for parents where the students served dessert and orally explained the plating design.

When the unit was shared with the teacher education class, the cohort was struck by the mindfulness of the preservice student's artistic choices. She came for meetings no less than three times and worked through multiple drafts of her curriculum unit. She followed an interest and learned how to edit her work in alignment with the realities of the assignment demands. She grew to understand the strength that research brings to instructional decision-making and experienced the important classroom metric that interpolates time with objective. Since teachers will not have time for everything, some content or activity will have to go. She learned how to use intuition to make bold cuts, understanding with the creative arts (which good teaching always is) that less is often more.

CREATIVE EXPRESSION IS NOT HARD TO EVALUATE

Too many teachers give generic, bland praise for creative efforts. What makes one student's work creative and another's less so? Preservice students often enter teacher education with the bias that it is inappropriate to "grade" artwork. After all, some people can draw better than others, so how fair is it to evaluate their creative achievement against those who are less talented? Yet, would one ever, *ever* use that logic in a discussion of math or literacy?

Indeed, Eisner (2001, p. 179) offers a harsh rebuke: "To abandon assessment and evaluation in education, regardless of the field, is to relinquish professional responsibility." Teachers can assess based on two dimensions: assignment criteria and artistry. First, did the project meet the required criterion? (Did the student groups compose a three- to five-minute stomp inspired by Zasuk's *The Book Thief* (2007) using all members of the group?) Second, what about the artistry of the work? To discuss artistry, Eisner points to the teacher's role as an educational connoisseur who evaluates three dimensions: technique (To what degree has the student handled the material with control and understanding?), inventiveness (Does the work say something new or say something familiar in a new way?), and expressive power (What is the aesthetic impact of the piece?). Specific rubrics, forms, or checklists are aligned with the criteria of the assignment to formalize and preserve the documentation of feedback.

The student must also be part of the assessment process. This is essential for the individual to develop mindfulness and perspective about his/her own learning trajectory, as well as provide the teacher with information she/he may not otherwise know about clarity of the assignment, challenges with the materials, or interpersonal group dynamics. "It is possible for a student to work on a project that he or she decided to discard and that, from the perspective of the product alone, looks like a failure . . . what needs attention in assessment and evaluation is not only manifest behavior, but also the kind of thinking that went into the project" (Eisner, 2001, p. 192). Brief interview protocols, individual conferences, or self-assessment forms are useful in securing this information.

Veteran math professor Herbert Ginsburg (2012) of Teachers College, Columbia University, explains six important words teachers need to carry with them at all times: "How did you get that? Why?" Teachers need to understand the student thinking that leads to outcomes. In every field, creative expression should inspire rich, informative feedback that propels teacher guidance, student growth, and tighter instructional design.

CREATIVITY REQUIRES PERSISTENCE, RESILIENCE, AND INCREASED COMFORT WITH FAILURE

Wayne Gretzky once said, "You miss 100% of the shots that you don't take." But, failure and rejection smart and can generate painful, lasting wounds. This is especially true for insecure children or adults who defy their nature to push beyond their comfort zones. Costa and Kalick (2010) have proposed a list of 16 habits of mind important for 21st-century educational success, notably "persisting" (stick with it), "managing impulsivity" (take your time), and "thinking about your own thinking" (metacognition). To this set, resilience, the ability to dust yourself off and move on after disappointment, seems appropriate. The creative process is perfumed by originality, which means that the creator stretches herself/himself beyond typical normative patterns. Yet, not all creative endeavors are equally successful or appreciated by the culture of the time. History is replete with examples of great artists (Amedeo Modigliani), authors (Herman Melville), and musical composers (Franz Schubert) who only gained renown posthumously.

How does one teach a child to deal with disappointment? At the 2012 Summer Olympic Games in London, U.S. gymnast Jordyn Wieber was unable to compete in the women's all-around competition because she finished third in the qualifying heat; only the top two qualifiers from each country move on to the final. She was the reigning world champion and had dedicated years to the pursuit of an Olympic medal. The moment was heartbreaking, but she pulled herself together and moved on. She is currently head coach of the Arkansas Razorbacks gymnastics team. Examples abound in every field of people who take risks that don't pan out. Children need to learn that there is no shame in trying your best and coming up short. The message is simple:

"It just didn't turn out the way I thought it would. And that's it. I could go on and on, but that's it." Creativity, by nature of its inherent risk, requires a supportive guard rail. Teachers and parents should not neglect the development and maintenance of this mental balustrade.

CREATIVITY CROSSES ALL DISCIPLINES, INCLUDING PEDAGOGY

Too often teachers parrot, "Be creative!" without any sense of what creativity looks like in their own field. We need to encourage teachers to provide students with real examples of creativity in multiple disciplines and encourage them to be creative themselves. They should be role models of creativity for their students, not individuals who only do things one way without ever laying bare the process of trying something new; however, within an educational landscape fixated on improving standardized test scores and publicizing evaluations, teachers may not feel safe diverging from prescriptive curricular lessons touted to ensure success for all and leave no child behind. As Diane Ravitch once claimed, "Mathematics and science work according to the same principles regardless of the city, state, or nation. The airplane that just flew over my home doesn't care what country it is in; it works the same in Austria, Nigeria, and Japan as it does in the United States" (Olson, 1998, p. 25).

However, people are infinitely more complex than machines. And it has never been true in education that every method or material works for every child in every city in every school in exactly the same way. Flexibility, insight, intuition, and improvisation have always been in the teacher's tool kit. We must work together to create an ecological model of classroom life where the desire for high standards and proficiency can coexist with creativity. Horace Mann reminds us, "Teaching is the most difficult of all arts, and the profoundest of all sciences," (cited in Cremin, 1957, p. 21). The dual nature of effective pedagogy recommends best practices and creative interruptions. Teacher educators can encourage future teachers to honor and hone both instincts. Schools should recognize that respect for the discipline and stretching boundaries energizes the instructional atmosphere.

There are limitless ways effective teachers demonstrate creativity in the classroom. The creative challenges of interdisciplinary curriculum design are one way to encourage teachers to think creatively about what it means to authentically integrate two disciplines. Inspired by the work of Jacobs (1989) and Fogarty and Pete (2009), in particular, teachers can deliberately grapple with fostering these connections. One teacher organized the classroom jobs in early September with economic content knowledge about Labor Day, including such concepts as division of labor, resources, and scarcity. Another devised a sixth-grade interdisciplinary math and history unit that merged medieval history and architecture as students designed blueprints for their own castle. The criticism of interdisciplinary work is thus: Let them master the basics of teaching math or literacy before muddying the waters. The answer is grounded in the development of sharper cognition: How can we expect teachers to promote flexible thinking if we don't give them opportunities to challenge their own creative juices?

CONCLUSION

"The ideal of using the present simply to get ready for the future contradicts itself. It omits, and even shuts out, the very condition by which a person can be prepared for his future" (Dewey, 1938/1977, p. 49). We know not what affordances and challenges this century will bring. It may take a dash of chutzpah to argue for reframing creativity as an important and multidimensional capacity in today's classrooms and teacher education programs. The time to halt the repetitive mantra of testing, testing, and more testing to know what a student knows is on the horizon. It is time to bravely stretch our wings and reinvigorate our intentions. Creativity should never be an excuse for ignoring directions or be reserved for the talented few; it can and should be part of the standards-based educational discourse today in both schools and teacher education programs. Creativity should be out of the box and between the lines. This chapter underscores five considerations to promote creativity in classrooms and schools for today and tomorrow. It will require school-wide support, parental advocacy, teacher buy-in, teacher education savvy, and national policy sensitivity, but isn't that always the way?

REFERENCES

Costa, A., & Kalick, B. (2010). It takes some getting used to: Rethinking curriculum for the 21st century. In H. H. Jacobs (Ed.), *Curriculum 21: Essential education for a challenging world* (pp. 210–26). Alexandria, VA: ASCD.

Cremin, L. (Ed.). (1957). *The republic and the school: Horace Mann on the education of free man*. New York: Teachers College Press.

Dewey, J. (1938/1977). *Experience and education.* New York: Simon & Schuster. (Original work published in 1938.)

Eisner, E. (2002). *The arts and the creation of mind.* New Haven, CT: Yale University Press.

Fogarty, R., & Pete, B. (2009). *How to integrate the curricula,* 3rd ed. Thousand Oaks, CA: Corwin.

Ginsburg, H. (2012, July 19). Advances in research on learning and its application. In J. James (Moderator), *Connecting advances in learning research and teacher practice: A conference about teacher education.* Teachers College, Columbia University, and Teaching Works, University of Michigan Symposium, conducted at Teachers College, Columbia University, New York, New York.

Jacobs, H. H. (1989). *Interdisciplinary Curriculum Design.* Alexandria, VA: ASCD.

Olson, S. (1989, September 30). Science friction. *Education Week 18*(4), pp. 24–29.

Zasuk, M. (2007). *The book thief.* New York: Random House.

Chapter Eight

Sifting the Metaphor

Teaching as a Culinary Art

USING THE CULINARY METAPHOR TO ENHANCE EDUCATIONAL PROFESSIONALISM

Just as the public can distinguish between home cook and master chef, so too can one highlight the distinction between the notion that anyone can teach and having a professionally trained and credentialed teacher. The rise of the Food Network and the Cooking Channel, as well as the proliferation of cooking videos, blogs, TV shows, and websites, coupled with the acclaim of celebrity chefs and social media influencers, has fostered a cognitive shift with respect to culinary arts. Given the wide acceptance of this distinction, this chapter develops the analogy between education and cooking with the aim of deepening the respect and understanding of teachers and their special-ized craft.

There are various reasons given for the lackluster glow afforded to the field of education. Philip Jackson (1990, p. 5) relates that by grade 7, chil-dren have spent 7,000 hours, or one-tenth, of their lives in the classroom. Adding middle and high school hours to the calculation builds what Lortie (1975/2002, p. 61) calls an "apprenticeship of observation" that may foster a mindset toward teaching as a form of simple, unscientific, and unskilled labor that anyone can do. Many feel that all you need to be a good teacher is to love children. Moreover, our own contemporary approaches to teacher education may generate an adverse impression of the profession. Quite honestly, if teaching only involves reading a script or following a set of high-leverage strategies, we may be needlessly tarnishing our own brand. This chapter considers an atypical approach to thinking about pedagogy through the metaphor of teaching as a culinary art to restore some polish and panache.

There are several distinct dimensions that organically frame the comparison. First, *a lesson plan is similar to a recipe*. There are ingredients, sequence matters, and the notation on paper is no substitute for the experience. Second, *the quality of the ingredients matters*. Ripe, fresh, local ingredients amplify the sauce in a way tired, preservative-laden packaged goods cannot. Third, *there are scientific and artistic dimensions to preparation and implementation*. Cooking, like teaching, requires precise scientific measurements of time and capacity, and qualitative attributes significantly transform the presentation. Consider how elegantly plating and serving the layer cake parallels the seamless way effective teachers prep and distribute materials.

Fourth, *assessment and evaluation of outcome data matters*. Whose meatloaf was left over at the potluck? Are the children eating nutritional food with enough variety? Did using a different brand of cocoa affect its taste? Likewise, what strategy was employed to hook learners into discussion of first amendment rights? What did they learn from the experience and how do you know? Finally, *both teachers and chefs work in conditions of extreme pressure bumping up against inflexible deadlines*. The restaurant opens at 6:00 p.m.; school ends at 3:40 p.m. There is little wiggle room and high uncertainty (fire drills, absences, walk-throughs, tech glitches, etc.), which privileges just-in-time problem solving and improvisation. So, while most people can get dinner on the table before bedtime, there are profound differences between those endeavors and the work of the professionally trained chef working in a professional establishment. Developing the comparison between master chef and master educator may enable deeper understanding and respect for specialization and professionalism of educators. *Now, after me, please . . .*

THE LESSON PLAN AS RECIPE

Like recipes, lesson plans vary in detail and format; however, the discourse of both forms of technical writing is precise with clear categories and specific syntax. Just as recipes have ingredients and steps, to lesson plans have materials, resources, and procedures. Timing and flexibility are key components of both. If the macaroni and cheese is browning on top, cover it with foil and lower the temperature or remove it from the oven a few minutes early. Likewise, when the lesson plan is not going smoothly, there are various steps the teacher can take to address the situation. The plan or the recipe is the starting point; it provides the structure and outlines the sequence, but the chef adjusts the cooking depending on the particular conditions and factors that affect the process. The professional knows how to tweak the recipe to improve the outcome.

QUALITY INGREDIENTS

Prepackaged, processed products cannot compete with fresh, local food sources. The composition and production of the food contributes to its value, flavor, and nutrition. Poor resources degrade the final product and long-term benefits. Similarly, rich, quality educational resources, works of art, inspired literature, or well-designed web quests provide balanced and vital nutrients for 21st-century growth and development. Today, a plethora of resources and choices in virtual and live arenas makes educational decision-making difficult. Valid and reliable sites offer security and trustworthiness, but it is all too easy to get sucked into flashy displays and trendy choices that don't provide long-term meaning or lasting fulfillment. Professionals know how to clarify this distinction. Master teachers understand the technical nature of the Common Core Standards, the academic language that crystallizes the lesson objective, and how to embed developmentally appropriate material that will engage learners with motivating, relevant, and healthy content.

> It is no reflection upon the nutritive quality of beefsteak that it is not fed to infants. It is not an invidious reflection upon trigonometry that we do not teach it in the first or fifth grade of school. It is not the subject *per se* that is educative or conducive to growth" (Dewey, 1938/1977, p. 46).

The professionals of the culinary arts and pedagogic arts have deep knowledge of the discipline that secures mindful selection, combination, and integration of high-quality, age-appropriate resources.

SCIENCE AND ART

Complex chemical reactions and mathematical proportions inform the scientific dimensions of the culinary arts. Likewise, plating, decor, and service add artistry to the gustatory experience. This duality is also found in the

classroom, where principles of behavioral conditioning, cognitive development, instructional design, and theories of motivation provide clinically rich
pedagogy, while sensitivity and nuance govern management, relationships
and classroom atmosphere. When to roast or sauté the asparagus? When to
use behaviorist, constructivist, or experientialist teaching to launch the lesson
on immigration? Technique and practice are directly informed by scientific
and artistic considerations. Teaching after afternoon recess is different from
teaching at 10:00 a.m., and teaching 35 students differs from teaching 12.
Furthermore, the way capable chefs make substitutions for individuals with
allergies or medical conditions echoes instructional differentiation for diverse learners. Professionals use research-based best practices, specialized
tools, and intuition born from experience to address particular needs with
aplomb, care, dignity, and responsibility. Professionals understand that both
artistry and science augment high-quality performance and outcome.

TIERS OF EVALUATION

Both restaurants and schools have multiple tiers of assessment, and regular
periodic evaluation can provide feedback to inform performance. Data is
gathered both informally and formally. At one end is the query, "How did
you like your meal?" At the other end is the standardized department of
health grading system or published restaurant review. Likewise, "How was
school today?" contrasts sharply with the state assessment and accountability
measures that rank districts, schools, administrators, and teachers. Poor rat-
ings may mean termination for professionals of either stripe. Evaluation is
integral to the economic and professional success of the practitioner and the
larger institution.

Yet, there is another pivotal factor that belies standardized evaluation:
preference. We like the things we like because we like them. People have
unique palates and learning profiles. To one individual the soup is too salty;
to another it is just right. In tandem, skip counting may be effective to
develop multiplication automaticity with one youngster, but arrays might be
more effective for another. Not everyone learns or tastes in the same way,
and so there is a subjective, personal, and quirky aspect of assessment and
evaluation that is lost in our search for patterns and trends. Let us not forget
the role of self-assessment either. Reflection on one's choices, both successes
and failures, is pivotal to understanding outcomes. Did the bread fail to rise
because the yeast was old? Did the student zone out because he is dealing

with a sick parent at home and cannot focus? Evaluation in both fields must seek to authentically combine contextual information with measurement data.

HIGH-PRESSURE ENVIRONMENTS

The principal is observing you and the projector is broken. You had planned to use the SMART Board to show a BrainPOP video as an advance organizer to your unit on amphibians and reptiles. She is coming in ten minutes. Teachers have to constantly adapt to the fluid and complex nature of classroom life. They have to think on their feet and make just-in-time changes to address the learning environment. Teachers need to plan for the unexpected. Lesson plans include a "What If?" category to enable anticipation of problems and misconceptions. As Julia Child (2006, p. 71) quipped, "Maybe the cat has fallen into the stew, or the lettuce has frozen, or the cake has collapsed. *Eh bien, tant pis"* (Oh well, too bad).

The nature of problem-solving tasks that both teachers and chefs face often requires an immediate response. One cannot say, "Let me think about it and I'll get back to you" when two children are arguing over a seat on the rug or a waiter walks out on the job. The immediacy and variability of the environment propel decision-making and improvisation to the forefront. "One of the secrets, and pleasures, of cooking is to learn to correct something if it goes awry; and one of the lessons is to grin and bear it if it cannot be fixed" (Child, 2006, p. 242). Professionals have the confidence and know-how to manage dynamic and complex environments.

CONCLUSION

A master teacher with years of experience hung the following quote above her blackboard: "Learning is a lifelong process." Both learning and eating are processes vital to existence, growth, and long-term health of individuals and communities. Dewey (1902/1956, p. 9) speaks of the similarity between the two: "Subject-matter is but spiritual food, possible nutritive material." The professional chef and the professional educator guide us toward refining our capacities and experiences to care for our families and ourselves.

What unique perspective does this analogy between cooking and teaching offer? It allows us to embrace the notion that we all teach and that professional teachers are at the end of the continuum that spans from novice to expert. This continuum contextualizes practice as part of—and not external to—life. In a sense, we are all teachers. To divorce the profession from common-sense understandings that parents, clergy, and many others teach seems unnecessarily awkward. Thinking about the spectrum from home cook to master chef may help revitalize the professionalization of teaching by situating the master teacher in context. "The aim is to open dialogue and extend horizons rather than to achieve closure around an all-embracing perspective" (Morgan, 1997, p. 8). Further development of this metaphor is encouraged to restore promise and reclaim respect for our educational professionals. Bon appétit!

REFERENCES

Child, J. (2006). *My life in France*. New York: Knopf.
Dewey, J. (1902/1956). *The child and the curriculum*. Chicago: University of Chicago Press. (Original work published in 1902.)
Dewey, J. (1938/1977). *Experience and education*. New York: Simon & Schuster. (Original work published 1938.)
Jackson, P. (1990). *Life in classrooms*. New York: Teachers College Press.
Morgan, G. (1997). *Images of organization*. Thousand Oaks, CA: Sage.

Chapter Nine

"More Beauty in a Rock"

What We Don't Teach and How It Matters

HOW TO OVERCOME THE NULL CURRICULUM BY ATTENDING TO QUALITATIVE DETAIL

What is curriculum? Curriculum is commonly defined as the content of study in a classroom during a set period of time, for example, a course, an academic year, or throughout K–12 schooling. Curriculum is derived from the Latin word that means racecourse, like a horse-racing track. One semester in the classroom management and instruction course, a question was posed to the teacher candidates: How is curriculum like a racecourse? The students had some interesting observations:

> One student said that it makes sense because thinking of curriculum as a racetrack implies that there is one set course of study, one path that everyone has to follow, in precisely the same way.
>
> Another said that the one who goes fastest wins, like the one who does the classwork the fastest. Another student chimed in that it is interesting that the fastest group is called the "accelerated track."
>
> Someone else said that only the first three finishers matter, only the top place wins the prize, like the ones with the high scores win the scholarship, and the rest are "left in the dust."
>
> Another student echoed this sense of schooling being an individual competition, where we are always pitting our performance against that of our peers.

To further understand curriculum, it is important to introduce some theory to ground our understanding of curriculum in schooling and education. Both terms, *schooling* and *education*, are intentional, and they are not synonymous. The following story illustrates a core distinction between the two concepts:

> My Zayde (Yiddish word for grandfather) taught me how to use a hammer when I was about seven years old. He had been teaching my brother, and I thought it only fair that he teach me too. Watching closely, he remarked, "You hammer like lightning." I thought he was complimenting me on my force, thinking of the powerful sound of thunder that typically accompanies the brilliant display of light. So, I smiled. "What do you mean?" I asked, waiting for him to elaborate further on my praise. "Well," he smirked, "lightning never hits in the same place twice."

This was an introduction to confirmation bias and hearing what one wants to hear. It is also an example of education outside the context of schooling. Everyone has memories of important moments of learning that happened outside of school. So, while schools are frequently castigated for not doing enough and missing the important lessons, remember that schools are not solely responsible for education, nor should they ever be. Parents, grandparents, communities, and peers have important roles in the development of an individual's education. Education occurs both inside and outside academic institutions. Now then, what, therefore, is schooling?

We typically think of schooling as encompassing those other elements of education, outside of the subject matter one learns throughout their time in school organizations. For example, schooling is learning what kind of shoes are cool to wear or what phrases you can say at recess to your friends but not the teacher or the administration. Schooling is learning which teachers will accept late papers or how to look like you are paying attention while really on your phone in class (which no one has really yet mastered). Schooling fills in those dimensions of social, cognitive, and behavioral learning in a school organization outside academic content and skills, enabling students to navigate norms, policies, and overall culture of the system and come out relatively unscathed.

Theoretically, when we think about curriculum, one must also consider context. Joseph Schwab (1973), prominent curriculum theorist, advances what he calls the four commonplaces of education: teacher, student, subject matter, and environment (milieu). Schwab asserts that every educational encounter contains these four elements: teacher, student, subject matter, context. To understand the separate impact of each, one can evaluate the consequences if a change is made in only one of the elements while the others are kept constant:

> If we move the learning outside because it is a beautiful, sunny day, and thereby change the context, we may have the same students, teacher, and subject matter, but some students will prefer to pick grass and see shapes in the clouds, activities that significantly alter the learning outcomes.
>
> If a teacher is absent and the substitute teacher is in charge for the day, while everything else stays the same, the students may experience a free-for-all, unless the principal is subbing that day!
>
> When a student is placed in a classroom with someone who has mocked them on social media or a student has entered the classroom midyear having moved from another location, the learning experience is likewise affected. The population of students influences the learning; thus, teaching is never a static enterprise no matter how many times the teacher has taught sixth grade mathematics in the same school.
>
> Lastly, let's change the subject matter content. One class learns about the Revolutionary War and the ensuing struggles to start up the new nation from the textbook alone, while another class complements the textbook study by listening to and analyzing the songs from the Broadway musical *Hamilton*. Changing the subject matter resources affects the learning experience.

Schwab's four commonplaces remind us that curriculum is infinitely flexible and larger than the content outline distributed on back-to-school night. Not only do the subject matter, objectives, standards, and core concepts of the lesson influence the educational experience, but also the other aspects of learning (teacher, fellow students, place) significantly modify the outcomes. When people are searching for schools for their children or teachers are researching job opportunities, they should look beyond printed promotional materials and website resources. As recommended in chapter 5, remember to walk the building, visit the bathrooms, listen to the way the students talk and walk between classes, and observe how the teachers and administrators greet one another.

John Dewey (1938/1977, p. 26), the eminent educational philosopher, writes in his classic work, *Experience and Education*, "How many students, for example, were rendered callous to ideas, and how many lost the impetus to learn because of the way in which learning was experienced by them?" Thus, Schwab avers that when we speak about curriculum, we have to be honest and contextualize our understanding of teaching and learning with other factors that definitively affect education. It is never subject matter alone that determines curriculum.

In addition, as also described in chapter 5, Elliot Eisner (2002, p. 159), influential arts education scholar and proponent, coined the curious concept of "null curriculum." He argues that what is not taught, the omissions and deletions, what is intentionally or unintentionally left out of pedagogy, matters. Let's recall that Eisner situates the null curriculum in a series of three related concepts: explicit curriculum, implicit curriculum, and null curriculum.

Explicit Curriculum

This is the official school curriculum as promulgated on the curriculum frameworks, websites, and formal school documentation, including lesson plans, homework assignments, and conversations with school personnel. Of course, this is the intended education, the education that is planned, not what actually happens. For example, the schedule reads that students have computers for the last period of the day; however, in reality many students actually leave school early because they are only working on yearbook during this time and would rather work on their home computer. So, the class may be "happening," technically, but only a handful of students are in the classroom.

Implicit Curriculum

This is the curriculum that emerges from the covert messages, aesthetic codes, social norms, and general classroom or school ambience. For example, are the messages posted on the school office outdated? Who gets to park in the school parking lot? Do some faculty have reserved spots? The implicit curriculum pays attention to the dynamics of power, control, and authority in school organizations.

> One day I was teaching fifth grade in a boys' yeshiva in New York City. When I came in, a student said to me, "Miss Ungar, the rebbe (Jewish studies teacher) wants you to take down the poster you put up about Albert Einstein." Now, I am thinking in my head, why? He is such an important icon of Jewish contribution to the world; he is a truly inspiring intellectual figure. Why am I

being asked to remove his image? And I am getting my ire up. So, I ask the student more about this directive. And he tells me that the picture of Einstein is bigger than the picture of the famous rabbis that the rebbe has put up. Ah, I think in my head, so while I may disagree with this teacher, it is clear he is talking about implicit curriculum. The rebbe thinks that the larger image of Einstein will implicitly convey that Einstein is more important than the scholars with smaller pictures.

Null Curriculum

This refers to what is not taught, what is absent from the school program, "what students in schools never have the opportunity to learn" (Eisner, 2002, p. 159). For example, does the school integrate U.S. history and world history, or are they taught as if they don't overlap? How do the students learn about Thanksgiving? Do they learn about Japanese internment camps? Do students know what to do when they have a friend who is cutting herself? Do students understand that there are different kinds of democracies? Do schools allow for authentic assessments or do teachers only give tests and quizzes? Are the arts taught in a rigorous way, or are they sidelined in clubs and after-school options? Do children know how to make responsible choices about their future career plans, carefully considering the profession they should pursue? Is maintaining mental and physical health an integrated part of the curriculum? The questions go on and on.

Nel Noddings (2009), an educational scholar who made significant contributions in the area of morality and the ethic of care, imagines a missing dimension in education in the humorous but woefully ironic dialogue (referenced earlier in chapter 6 in relation to listening) between a visitor from another world and a representative educator, appropriately named "Ed."

> The visitor comments: "It struck me as odd that, although your people spend much of their time in homemaking, parenting, and recreation, these topics are rarely addressed in your schools." Ed dismisses the visitor's comments with refutations about full schedules and the improper intrusion of these topics into school life. (p. 436)

Each individual can answer the question, "What was not included in your education, and how did that omission affect your life?" Some may wish they sewed better, could change a tire, or were more comfortable using power tools. It could be they wish to manage stress better, organize data more efficiently, or calculate probabilities faster. Eisner's message is that what is not taught in schools impacts the student's future in real ways. Before moving on, let's summarize the essential understandings or big ideas from the curriculum theory:

1. School is only one educational context. Learning is a lifelong process that also exists outside school walls.
2. Curriculum is modified by the teacher, the students in the classroom, the subject matter choices, the teaching method, and the environment.
3. What is not taught matters.

Next, let's dive deeper into the third claim to consider what is not taught in our schools, and the implications of these omissions. What are the consequences of curricular choices and omissions?

There are many ways to answer this question, but this chapter is concerned with regard to the null curriculum in education that looms large over several concrete areas. The focus in the next section is discrimination, not the how word is typically used, in terms of tolerance, stereotyping, or overcoming biases, but discrimination as the practice of discernment, of noticing deeply. When one speaks of noticing deeply, we are really talking about gathering evidence, forming opinions, and making judgments. We are talking of the nuanced space where a person has to figure out what they truly think, based on their mental faculties and sensory experiences, leading to an evaluation or decision.

So, what does it mean to discern, to notice qualitative detail and sensory elements, and why the concern that we are not advancing this skill in our educational organizations and institutions today? Benjamin Bloom, father of what is called the taxonomy of educational objectives, developed a hierarchy of cognitive tasks from lower order to higher order. They move from straight repeat-after-me, recall-of-knowledge tasks, to comprehension, understanding the knowledge, to application, representing the content in a display or multistep task, followed by analysis, taking things apart, and synthesis, putting things back together in a novel way. On top of his hierarchy is the skill of evaluation. Anderson and Krathwohl (2001) modified Bloom and Krathwohl's 1956 version, and one of their critiques of the original model asks why evaluation is at the top of the hierarchy. It is easy to like or dislike something; how is that more advanced cognitively than building a robot or analyzing Emily Dickinson's poetry? What was the thinking behind Bloom and Krathwohl's (1956) original taxonomy?

The answer is that evaluation is defined as the process of discernment based on criteria from the experts in the field. Evaluation is understood from the perspective of an educated reviewer who evaluates a new piece of music, a book, or a building, not from the perspective of a first-time novitiate. There is a presumption underlying evaluation that one has studied the field deeply and is basing his/her evaluation on what is valued in the field. In this age of bloggers and influencers who rise to prominence, often without what used to be called formal education, one must still admit that their evaluation is based on evidence, criteria that they use to offer insight about the pros and cons, strengths and weaknesses, and affordances and limitations based on autodidactic practices.

Discernment is thus a judgment call, and we want our children to make decisions throughout their lives from a place of knowledge, not from peer pressure, and certainly not only from YouTubers or social media influencers. Even if one frequently reads the customer reviews before purchasing something, we still want individuals to actively render their own decisions and be able to articulate the justification. And let's remember that there are more important decisions in life than online comparison shopping.

Aaron Fried (2007) wrote a powerful article entitled "Are Our Children Too Worldly?" In this article he concludes, "They are not worldly enough." His argument is that if children are not exposed to the finest forms of culture and encouraged to develop interests in fields that matter to them, when the gates and fences that block access open, they will make a mad dash for the crassest and lowest forms of flashy entertainment. "Our children," he writes, "should be made aware of the existence of the 'low' and 'high' culture in the world out there" (p. 59). If we teach them the whole world is decadent, he explains, we are not only inviting rebellion, we are depriving them of deepening and expanding their interests. In addition, he warns that if we want to replace influence from the lowest denominator of secular culture with perspectives from the finest and most venerated in the fields of interest, we need to be proactive in making that happen. Making connections between the child's interest and the larger field of their interest is a job for educators—the parents and teachers.

This concern about null curriculum in education relates to the development of discernment, the ability to determine appropriate and inappropriate, refinement versus crassness, quality versus tacky. Whatever the field, be it music, art, product design, architecture, sports, or film, are we providing children the tools to discern, to determine for themselves, that this is inferior or this is a quality resource from which to learn. Are we raising them to make selections that advance thinking, growth, and development? Even in virtual environments, which influencers, bloggers, or podcasts are worthwhile to follow and why?

Now let's be clear, what is profane, prurient, or developmentally inappropriate is not the same for every population, and there are gray areas. It is vital to support individuals by cultivating interests, without making policy statements that everyone has to study gymnastics or acapella music. Interests or pursuits that are internally motivated, not for school grades, are crucial to maintaining good mental health and finding joy in life. How do children figure out what makes them happy and satisfied without opportunities to explore healthy, appropriate, quality interests? Should children be exposed to the finest in every field, and who decides what that is? For example, if they are really interested in photography, do we guide them to Matthew Brady's civil war photographs or to those of Jacob Riis, with his images of the LE side tenement life? Do we include the work of Gordon Parks or Imogene Cunningham? How do we allow opportunity for students to follow their interests and learn how to distinguish what is of value in the fields that matter to them in a balanced but not heavy-handed way? Let us also not forget that real, authentic, firsthand experiences need to outweigh virtual lest we become the couch potato human of the *WALL E* (2008) film. For example, with young children, planting a seed should take precedence over watching the slow-motion digitization of plant growth.

There is a rich and deep tradition in every area of a child's interest. "It is a development of experience and into experience that is really wanted" (Dewey, 1902/1956, p. 18). How can teachers and parents engender this skill of noticing deeply? The "one and done" ethos of trying and discarding activities and interests sheds persistence and commitment to satisfying pursuits like reptiles slithering from desiccated skin. The quest for adventure, novelty, and excitement, moving rapidly to the next "cool" thing, deprives children and adults of the satisfaction of the deep dive into lifelong pursuits. Beyond "I like it" or "I didn't like it," how can educators promote the development of discernment, of critical insight that pushes beyond arbitrary whim? Frankly, do our students even know that they don't know?

Recently I added an online collaborative reading assignment to one of my courses where students have to post a comment to a short theoretical reading or respond to the comments of a peer. One week I posted something from Paulo Freire, a Brazilian educational philosopher who authored, among other works, a famous piece called *Pedagogy of the Oppressed*. The title of the chapter was "Reading the World/Reading the Word." It concerned the relationship between teaching and learning, and how teachers have to keep learning to keep teaching. Freire describes how teachers need to go back and forth between their knowledge of the content and their knowledge of their students to make sense of what is actually being learned. He discusses how teachers may need to modify their teaching for students to learn. One student commented that she doesn't like the word *reading* in the title.

Inquiry, critical thinking, and discussion in education is vital to learning; however, scholars in the field use the verb "reading" to address how humans make sense of the world around us. Have the humility to know that you may not know, so the point is, we have to teach students to not only like or dislike, but also understand that disciplines, knowledge, and scholarship exists in every field, and to really discern one needs to invest in understanding what the experts in the field theorize, conceptualize, and assert. Discernment is a skill, not just a happenstance opinion poll or survey monkey instrument. It is not liking something on Facebook.

Discernment is important not only in individual development, but also in terms of the environment. How does one select a community in which to live? What is important in the raising of children? Will the selected setting offer basic opportunities for social play and learning, and if not, how will this be supplemented? Children need to know how important not only selecting a spouse is, but also the necessity of weighing and considering the selection of the community and environment in which they will raise their own families. As cited in Schwab, context is an aspect of education. Thus, community is also an educational institution; where one lives critically affects educational opportunities and limitations.

Furthermore, there is a dark side to community life. Within communities, parents need to stop feeling threatened by other people's choices . For example, when parents of similarly aged children make different school selections, oftentimes another set of parents feels threatened by the alternative decision. It is as if because someone else has selected another path for their child, it somehow casts a shadow on one's own decision-making and sows seeds of doubt in the choice. If one has been careful in making the schooling decision, careful in reading the school, careful in examining the differences between institutions, careful with thinking of the child and his/her needs, then the legwork was completed correctly. Remember parents are also curriculum developers, and selection of community and school community will pro-

foundly influence life. Practice discernment, and do not allow peer pressure
to interfere with what is right for the child, the grandchildren, or one's self. If
we can stop thinking of curriculum as a racetrack, where the fastest child
wins, perhaps we can understand that every individual has a different path
and destination.

When asked about the best way to teach children to make decisions, the
answer is one has to allow them to make decisions. When teaching children
to discern, one has to not only arrange practice, but also teach what it means
to be an informed consumer, invest time in the examination process, inform
opinion with scholarship and evidence, and do research. Research means research, searching again, again, and again. The Hebrew word for question,
kasha, means questions, but it also means difficulty. Life presents us with
difficulties and questions. That is a given. One might say that is part of G-d's
curriculum for us. But it is our job as parents, teachers, concerned citizens,
and community members to provide our children with the tools to respond.
Discernment (noticing deeply), evaluation based on knowledge and research,
and the humility to acknowledge ignorance or misunderstandings are important instruments to sanely and safely make wiser decisions for oneself and
one's family. So, if it isn't taught in our schools, this omission can be addressed.

One strategy that has proven effective across multiple age groups is the
describe, analyze, interpret, and reflect model from the discipline of arts
education. Inspired by the work of Wolcott (1994) and Housen and Yenawine (2010), the sequence of the learning experience draws the child or student
close with an examination of the properties or attributes of the object or
event. This is followed by analytic inquiry that looks across the different
separate elements and considers them in an organized pattern. Next, the child
is asked about meaning or interpretation of the form and content. Lastly, the
child or student considers personal connection or relationships.

> I bring in my collection of rocks. They vary in size, shape, texture, color,
> weight, mineral composition, and place of origin. We begin the learning in a
> circle, and one at a time, I silently pass each rock from student to student. Then
> I put them all on a table that the class stands around. The class is asked, "What
> do you notice?" Students volunteer comments about characteristics. If a stu-
> dent points to one and says, "This one looks like tofu," I respond, "What did
> you see that makes you say that?" This returns the dialogue to description.
>
> After we have identified vital properties, including how some reflect light,
> some have sharp edges, and some feel chalky, I ask the class to organize the

set in an arrangement without telling the rest of the class their method of organization. We explore the organizing principles of shape, color, size, composition, etc. In doing so, we have framed our analysis in diverse ways and encouraged multiple ways of knowing.

Then, I ask them about the role of rocks in real life. How are rocks used in the world? Some responses: building materials, riverbeds, asphalt, irrigation, the Grand Canyon, gardens, sidewalks, sculpture, tectonic plates, pottery, hiking, archaeology, sand, diamonds, gems, and weapons.

Since the class is situated in a Jewish institution of higher education, the class is asked to reflect on rocks in terms of Judaism. Some responses:

There is a tradition of putting a rock on a grave when visiting.

The 10 Commandments were written on rock.

One of G-d's names is "Tzur" Rock (i.e., "Rock of Ages").

Jacob put a ring of rocks around his head before he had his dream (Genesis 28:11).

Moses hit the rock to get water (Numbers 20:11).

Joshua put 12 rocks in the Jordan River when he crossed it (Joshua 4:9).

Lastly, students are asked about their own experiences with rocks, and they speak about climbing mountains, skipping stones with siblings, building rock sculptures on the beach, painting rocks, reading about Paddington Bear and his rock garden, falling in love with Harry Potter and the "Sorcerer's Stone," building fires in summer camp, and wondering what the expression "between a rock and a hard place" truly means.

The session ends with the following quote from Elliot Eisner (2002, p. 85): "There is more beauty in a rock than any of us is likely to discover in a lifetime."

On the Jewish holiday Passover, a section of the Haggadah, the text read at the Passover Seder, asks those seated at the table to think about who is missing from the Seder table and invite them to join. Similarly, with the null curriculum, we think about what is missing from our schools and how we can integrate that into our lives and the lives of the next generation. The skill of discernment, of noticing deeply, is crucial in the development of healthy interests throughout life, fostering resilient and growth-oriented individuals, families, and communities. "Attention to the particular qualities of, say, a rock is not a customary mode of perception, yet there is more beauty in a rock than any of us is likely to discover in a lifetime" (Eisner, 2002, p. 85). Discernment, paying attention and giving mindful focus, is harder than ever, but perhaps that makes it all the more important as an essential skill to cultivate and refine.

REFERENCES

Anderson, L., & Krathwohl, D. R. (Eds.). (2001). *A taxonomy for learning, teaching, and assessing: A revision of Bloom's taxonomy of educational objectives.* Boston: Allyn & Bacon.

Bloom, B. S., and Krathwohl, D. R. (1956). *Taxonomy of educational objectives: The classification of educational goals,* by a committee of college and university examiners. Handbook I: The Cognitive Domain. NY: Longmans, Green & Co.

Dewey, J. (1902/1956). *The child and the curriculum.* Chicago: University of Chicago Press. (Original work published in 1902.)

Dewey, J. (1938/1977). *Experience and education.* New York: Simon & Schuster. (Original work published in 1938.)

Eisner, E. (2002). *The arts and the creation of mind.* New Haven, CT: Yale University Press.

Freire, P. (1970/2002). *Pedagogy of the oppressed,* 30th anniversary ed. New York: Continuum.

Fried, A. H. (2007). Are our children too worldly? *Hakirah: The Flatbush Journal of Jewish Law and Thought, 4,* 37–67.

Housen, A., & Yenawine, P. (2010). Basic VTS at a glance. *Visualthinkingstrategies.org.* Retrieved September 4, 2020, from https://www.licm.org/media/filer_public/e6/2f/e62fecc5-2e9c-4043-b04f-ffed33204dad/art_programs_download_basic-vts-at-a-glance.pdf.

Noddings, N. (2009). The aims of education. In D. Flinders & S. Thorton (Eds.), *The curriculum studies reader,* 3rd ed. (pp. 425–38). New York: Routledge. Reprinted from *Happiness and education,* pp. 74–93, by N. Noddings, 2003, Cambridge University Press.)

Schwab, J. J. (1973). The practical 3: Translation into curriculum. *School Review, 81*(4), 501–22. Retrieved September 7, 2020 from http://www.jstor.org/stable/1084423

Wolcott, H. F. (1994). *Transforming qualitative data: Description, analysis, and interpretation.* Thousand Oaks, CA: Sage.

Chapter Ten

Teach Like a Human

The Reality Gap in Educator Preparation[1]

SUPPORTING NEW TEACHER DEVELOPMENT FOR LIFELONG LEARNING

> You can't ever reach perfection, but you can believe in an asymptote toward which you are ceaselessly striving.—Kalanithi, 2016, p. 115

If you haven't read Paul Kalanithi's remarkable memoir *When Breath Becomes Air*, you must, for as it speaks about his untimely death, it also speaks about life, education, relationships, reality, and the role of uncertainty, which interfaces with all these elements. I have found this narrative of Kalanithi's life especially meaningful in reframing educator preparation.

Educational philosopher Maxine Greene advocates for teachers to routinely pose the question starter, "What if?" In addition to setting up exploration stations for science content or designing math games to teach fractions her perspective on education reminds educators to encourage students to imagine sights, sounds, and feelings; find language to express personal stories; and delight in the process of wondering without immediately regurgitating a correct answer in a proscribed formulaic fashion.

Last semester a student of mine in our educator preparation program (EPP) described her fieldwork in a New York City public school where she saw the following: The objective for the art class was for the learner to draw a pumpkin using crayons. "Now we know the Common Core has gone too far," the senior student teaching cohort rightly responded. Clearly, that our national curriculum is a topic of conversation among teacher candidates is a good thing. No doubt the Common Core Learning Standards (CCLS) have generated positive discussion regarding what is important for our nation's students to know and be able to do. And, as countless others have argued, unless we have such accountability measures as tests to measure student performance and progress, we are depriving parents, teachers, and taxpayers of valuable information about actual learning mastery with respect to the standards. The naysayers bemoan the diminishment of the arts, STEM problem-solving initiatives, teachable moments, and overall teacher professionalism with top-down strictures that threaten to strangle good teaching and learning. Coherent arguments frame both sides; however, there is a significant reality gap between educator preparation and educational practice. It may behoove education policy makers to be mindful of what they actually know and have experienced in their own lives as they make impactful decisions going forward.

A few points to ponder: Educator preparation will always be incomplete. Preparing for the future without living in the moment is illogical. Research-based effective strategies will not work for everyone at all times.

Educator preparation, like preparation in many fields, relies on simulation and approximation. Football players practice plays, and their coaches offer targeted feedback. Actors rehearse lines and block scenes, while directors offer critique and guide refinement. Yet, almost no one would argue that practice or rehearsal is an authentic substitute or stable predictor for the live game or performance. Similarly, those learning to become teachers begin by teaching model lessons in higher education classrooms, leading to full-semester student teaching practicums through clinical partnerships with local public and nonpublic schools. EPPs are exceedingly grateful to those institutions for opening their school communities to teacher candidates to learn from their master educators. But let's face it, there is nothing like the new teacher's first years. And as much as EPPs can work to align content, skill, and technique with what is happening in school classrooms, there is always a gap. Until the new teacher has to stand on his/her own without the support of the cooperating teacher and be responsible for everything from management to supplies, from prepping the instructional sequence to handling the tears, she/he will not know exactly what it is like to be a teacher. That reality check cannot be woven into the fabric of the EPP. Schools need to address this phase of educator preparation, and states need to fund comprehensive teacher development programs for first-year teachers. It is unrealistic and illogical for new teachers to be ready to go on day one as master teachers without having the experiences of the first few years. And these learning experiences are vital to the establishment of the educator's sense of mission and connection to children and school communities.

Our recent graduates are ready for their first year in the classroom; however, they are not as good as they will be by their third year in the classroom. And truth be told, they will not be well prepared for some of what they will face. Can anyone really project what issues, skills, policies, or challenges will take hold of classroom practice five years down the road? Yes, we know the technology will break down, which is why we teach future teachers to plan for that contingency. *How else could you teach this if the projector is not working?* Yes, we know some children will not understand what the denominator represents and how to address the misconception of a larger number always meaning more. *Which math manipulatives will support conceptual understanding for this child at this point in time?* We practice lockdown drills and encourage character development with socioemotional skill development. *How can we show Barbara that we are actively listening to her?* Yet, we, in EPPs, are not prophets who can see that far down the lane to know that coding is necessary for everyone to master or that cursive handwriting is truly passé.

It will always be important *to teach like a human*. Every effective and caring professional educator wants to help children have the best and widest platform to access opportunity; have a satisfying, productive, and meaningful life; and feel fulfilled when they reach their end of days. John Dewey, one of America's most preeminent educational philosophers, in his classic work *Experience and Education*, asserts, "How many students, for example, were rendered callous to ideas, and how many lost the impetus to learn because of the way in which learning was experienced by them?" (Dewey, 1938/1977, p. 26). Teaching is a complex and fascinating profession because each day is different, each year is different, and mornings in classrooms are so different from afternoons. Teaching requires balance and perspective, fluidity and stability, and competence and care. Teachers need to expect the unexpected while simultaneously crafting detailed plans, minute by minute. But they also need to make learning stimulating, imaginative, and alive. They may need CCLS math review packets, but they also need to consider how some leaf patterns map the Fibonacci series. They need to turn on students to the excitement of learning by integrating what's cool in the world now with things that may be of interest to them in the future. These practices cement relationships between teaching and living, learning and life, and one human being and another.

Lemov's *Teach Like a Champion: 49 Techniques That Put Students on the Path to College* (2010) details 49 strategies to improve the effectiveness of teaching and learning. According to one of our EPP's recent graduates, this book governs instructional practice in the charter school where she is currently teaching. While some of the techniques described by Lemov are similar to those included in other popular classroom management texts (Thompson, 2013; Wong & Wong, 2009), for example, "Do Now, "Check for Understanding," or "Exit Ticket," others are problematic when implemented at the lower elementary levels. For example, students may echo answers via technique 23, "Call and Response," without comprehension. On a visit to a graduate's classroom the following was observed:

> The grade 1 low-ability students were learning about 2D geometric shapes, and the teacher holds up a small plastic trapezoid while reading from a scripted lesson plan.
> "This is a trapezoid. A what?" she asks.
> "A trapezoid," the students answer.
> She continues, "A trapezoid has two parallel sides. A trapezoid has . . ."
> The students respond, "Two parallel sides."
> She goes on. "How many sides does a trapezoid have?"
> "Two," the students mimic without thinking or looking at the object she holds before them.

Teaching techniques and strategies must be tempered with firsthand local knowledge of the particular individuals involved and their unique learning needs and assets. As the example illustrates, mindlessly following scripts crafted by experts who do not know the children in the classroom is a recipe for disaster. Thus, while the title of this chapter mirrors the "Teach Like a Champion" mantra, compiling a list of techniques to address the perspective of "Teaching Like a Human" is not recommended. How many more lists, rubrics, guidelines, principles, standards, and benchmarks does the world actually need? Yet, it does seem important to set some margins and make connections with scholarship that textures the profession responsibly to balance out the data-driven, high-stakes corporate assessment measures currently strangling educator preparation.

As a starting point, this chapter advances four intersecting dimensions. First, teaching like a human includes risk-taking. "Indeed, the ideograph from the Chinese language that represents opportunity is the very same symbol as that which represents danger" (Barth, 2007, p. 217). To encourage risk-taking, Barth includes the following coupon, which has been adapted for preservice teachers. It states, "I blew it. I tried something new and innovative, and it didn't work as well as I wanted. This coupon entitles me to be free of criticism for my efforts. I'll continue to pursue ways to help our school/ classroom be successful" (Barth, 2007, p. 216).

In teacher education courses, the phrase "trying something new" minimizes the heroic and earth-shaking stress induced by the term *risk*, but the message is consistent. New teachers must put on the "oxygen mask of learning" (Barth, 2007, p. 214) and embrace the learning that comes from risk-taking.

Next, there is the related component of acknowledging missteps. Beyond the cute coupon lies the foundational ethics of owning up to incorrect factual statements and inappropriate emotional reactions. Unlike the Billy Collins poem "The History Teacher" (1999, p. 77–78), where "the Stone Age became the Gravel Age, named after the long driveways of the time," teachers should not err because of inadequate preparation. The must take care in modeling authentic remediation of misspeaks and missteps. "We are fallible, and should not pretend that we are anything else" (Sizer & Sizer, 1999, p. xviii). The messaging from such admission is potent:

> Yet because conveying accurate knowledge is one of the chief aims of teaching, errors of fact or interpretation must be candidly confessed, better methods than those previously used ought to be presented, and the significance of both should be explained. Not only is learning thus promoted and honesty exemplified, but perhaps more important, teachers themselves can be seen struggling to overcome the natural difficulties of learning, and their students can thus grow in understanding. (Banner & Cannon, 1997, p. 112)

Third, new teachers need to tread the adopt/adapt pathway (Posner, 2005, p. 24), recognizing the interplay between planned curriculum, enacted curriculum, and experienced curriculum (Gehrke, Knapp, & Sirotnik, 1992). Planned curriculum resides in curriculum guides, lesson plans, curriculum maps, and the teacher's mind, while enacted curriculum refers to the way the curriculum is "enacted by teachers in the classroom, although one is left with the quandary over whose account of enactment—students', teachers', or observers'—to believe" (Gehrke et al., 1992, p. 55). The experienced curriculum reflects the way the curriculum is received by students, honoring their individual and personal experience of the teaching and learning process. This reflective cycle encourages the development of habitual practices of mindfulness and gap analysis across the planning, implementation, and assessment processes.

Lastly, teaching like a human will require Greene's "wide-awakeness" to the world around us during the time in which we live. This book consciously mirrors Maxine Greene's practice of interleaving works of art and literature alongside personal experiences as exemplars of how to let the world and our encounters with its manifold creations be sources of inspiration, curiosity, and wonder.

> We see it as part of the human effort (so often forgotten today) to seek a greater coherence in the world. We see it as an effort to move individuals (working together, searching tougher) to seek a grounding for themselves so that they make break through the "cotton wool" of dailyness, passivity, and boredom, and awaken to the colored, sounding, problematic world (Greene, 2001, p. 7).

Encouraging personal connections and imaginative relationships between the arts and life nurtures identity and community.

Some years ago, several members of the New York Board of Regents convened a town hall-style meeting to discuss the New York State Teacher Certification Examinations (NYSTCE), which have arguably hijacked EPPs throughout the state. The candidates' pass scores not only serve to credential the particular teacher candidate, but also act as outcome measures for the EPP. Locally, in our program, like all programs, in addition to the New York state standardized measures, candidates are evaluated at the close of every semester on academic performance, professional dispositions, and pedagogic performance in the field. Feedback from cooperating teachers and fieldwork supervisors informs about the candidate's progress, and concerns are formally documented and addressed. One of the most important measures is summarized in the all-important dictum from TEAC, the Teacher Education Accreditation Council, which asks if the candidate practices "learning how to learn." This includes the following questions: Does the candidate accept critique with maturity? Does the candidate's performance demonstrate improvement across the model lesson sequence? Does the candidate communicate in a timely manner with professional academic language? Teaching like a human means we can all get better at what we do, that we learn how to learn from experience, and from mistakes one can learn a great deal about others and themselves. Of course we want our students to pass the NYSTCE, but those measures are inexact and incomplete predictors of pedagogic prowess.

In fact, as previously noted, it is vital for teacher candidates to remember what it is like to be confused, to fail, and to grapple with learning skills so they can help their own students with similar struggles. Yes, they should climb the asymptote to perfection, but they should also simultaneously enjoy the process of teaching and learning. The worry today is that the pressurized environment of educational settings derails strong prospective educators from entering the field and staying in the profession. The teacher shortages throughout the United States lend support to this claim. García and Weiss (2019), in a five-part report that is part of the Perfect Storm in the Teacher Labor Market Series, find that, "The teacher shortage is real, large, and growing, and worse than we thought." They cite working conditions and other factors that encourage educators to quit and dissuade people from entering the profession. Ironically, teachers also improve by teaching and learning, and learning is a lifelong process that shouldn't stop when schooling ends. Educators should be disposed to try new strategies and technologies throughout their careers.

One of the lessons from the life of Paul Kalanithi, who for years trained to become a neurosurgeon and neuroscientist, and never got to work long term in the position for which he was educated, reminds us of the value of making meaningful choices each day, despite the uncertainty of not knowing what the future will bring. In his powerful book, his life and the importance of his relationships with family and friends illustrate how the choices that determine our lives can inspire others. His oncologist repeatedly implored him to define his priorities, to determine his values. When education is not part of one's intended future but is valuable in and of itself, today, in this very moment, and those that follow, a radically different understanding of education and life takes shape. This is precisely where educational philosophy can inform educational policy. Teaching like a human means acknowledging limits while redefining aspirations in an uncertain environment. What if we all gave this some thought? How can this insight infuse educator preparation with realism, dignity, humility, and humanity so our future teachers continue to want to learn how to educate more effectively?

In addition to the four aspects introduced earlier, this chapter concludes by offering two practical suggestions to initiate further application of what it could mean to "teach like a human" and how this orientation can inform educator preparation. First, teacher educators should consider integrating current events into teacher education courses so candidates have an opportunity to dialogue about pivotal and provocative events and issues swirling around them. Journell (2013) argues that more alarming than the overwhelming lack of civic and political knowledge by preservice teachers is the underlying dispositional limitation. "At the crux of these findings is an alarming lack of intellectual curiosity among preservice teachers" (p. 342). The nature of current events favors just-in-time, in the moment, working through real concerns from competing perspectives.

Discussions about current events force teacher candidates to authentically reflect and examine their ideas against the backdrop of different opinions and emotions. Bafumo and Noel (2014) detail specific technology-based integrative strategies to enhance consistent current events learning by preservice teachers. Learning how to dialogue, listen, empathize, support claims with evidence, and evaluate media bias, personal assumptions, and intuitive calculations is good "practice" for the vibrant life, global awareness, and democratic discourse we want to see in every classroom (Haas & Laughlin, 2000). As Dewey (1938/1977, p. 49) reminds us, "We always live in the time we live and not at some other time, and only by extracting at each present time the full meaning of each present experience are we prepared for doing the same thing in the future. This is the only preparation that amounts to anything in the long run."

Second, teacher educators can encourage candidates to develop the gumption to reveal areas of weakness and find language to ask their cooperating teachers for assistance. Feiman-Nemser (2012) describes relationships with colleagues as one of three aspects of school life, especially salient for beginning teachers. She explains that as a result of the prevalent "sink or swim" first-year narrative in many bureaucratic school organizations, "teachers may feel reluctant to ask for help or share problems, believing that good teachers figure things out for themselves. Even if teachers do get together they may not know how to talk about teaching and learning in productive ways" (p. 158). If as candidates they can begin to feel comfortable identifying need and requesting guidance without fear of punitive devaluation or judgmental reprobation, perhaps they will continue to seek support and resources in their first few years and those that follow.

> Novices need opportunities to talk with others about their teaching, analyze students' work, examine problems, and consider alternative explanations and actions. If novices learn to talk about specific practices in specific terms, if

they learn to ask for clarification, share uncertainties, and request help, they will be developing skills and dispositions that are crucial in the ongoing improvement of teaching (Feiman-Nemser, 2001, p. 1030).

However, it is important to acknowledge the realistic constraints of classroom teaching today. Many preservice teachers and their supervisors report turf wars with cooperating teachers reluctant to give up teaching time for the novice to "practice." Burdened with multiple compliance documentation tasks and ongoing assessment and evaluation mechanisms, cooperating teachers struggle with their own heavy load of curricular expectations and professional responsibilities (Sadler, 2006; Zeichner, 2010). Most are passionate about sharing craft knowledge (Barth, 2006; Greene, 1984) but simply don't have the time to dedicate exclusively to candidate mentorship amid their primary professional obligations. Thus, teacher candidates need to bravely initiate and manage these important conversations to develop a sense of professional agency rather than waiting for traditional formal feedback sessions.

"The most important attitude that can be formed is that of desire to go on learning" (Dewey, 1938/1997, p. 48). There is a big push in education today to bring high-leverage practices up to scale (Schneider, 2014). Teaching like a human provides balance to this charge by addressing the individual and his/ her learning needs at a particular moment in time. The message of striving for life and learning, shared by Kalanithi (2016, p. 149), who found courage in Samuel Beckett's (1958/1997, p. 476) turn of phrase, "I can't go on. I'll go on," can embolden resolve as we press forward together to reframe educator preparation in this challenging and uncertain climate. In this way, educator preparation can be for both today and tomorrow, no matter which way the policy winds blow.

REFERENCES

Bafumo, M. E., & Noel, A. (2014). Using technology supported strategies to improve preservice teacher preparation in social studies. *Canadian Journal of Action Research, 15*(1), 40–49.

Banner, J. M., & Cannon, H. C. (1997). *The elements of teaching*. New Haven, CT: Yale University Press.

Barth, R. (2006). Improving relationships within the schoolhouse. *Educational Leadership, 63*(6), 8–13.

Barth, R. (2007). Risk. In M. Fullan (Ed.), *The Jossey-Bass reader on educational leadership*, 2nd ed. (pp. 211–18). San Francisco, CA: Jossey-Bass.

Beckett, S. (1958/1997). *Molloy Malone dies, the unnamable*. New York: Knopf.

Collins, B. (1999). The history teacher. In *Questions about angels*. Pittsburgh, PA: Pittsburgh University Press.

Dewey, J. (1938/1977). *Experience and education*. New York: Simon & Schuster. (Original work published in 1938.)

Feiman-Nemser, S. (2001). From preparation to practice: Designing a continuum to strengthen and sustain teaching. *Teachers College Record, 103*(6), 1,013–55.

Feiman-Nemser, S. (2012). *Teachers as learners*. Boston: Harvard Education Press.

García, E., & Weiss, E. (2019, March 26). The teacher shortage is real, large, and growing, and worse than we thought. Perfect Storm in the Teacher Labor Market Series. *EPI.org*. Retrieved July 16, 2019, from https://www.epi.org/publication/the-teacher-shortage-is-real-large-and-growing-and-worse-than-we-thought-the-first-report-in-the-perfect-storm-in-the-teacher-labor-market-series/.

Gehrke, N. J., Knapp, M. S., & Sirotnik, K. A. (1992). In search of the school curriculum. *Review of Research in Education, 18*, 51 110.

Greene, M. (1984). How do we think about our craft. *Teachers College Record, 86*(1), 55–67.

Greene, M. (2001). *Variations on a blue guitar: The Lincoln Center Institute lectures on aesthetic education*. New York: Teachers College Press.

Haas, M. E., & Laughlin, M. A. (2000). Teaching current events: Its status in social studies today. Paper presented at the Annual Conference of the American Educational Research Association, New Orleans, Louisiana, April 24–28.

Journell, W. (2013). What preservice social studies teachers (don't) know about politics and current events—and why it matters. *Theory & Research in Social Education, 41*(3), 316–51.

Kalanithi, P. (2016). *When breath becomes air*. New York: Random House.

Lemov, D. (2010). *Teach like a champion: 49 techniques that put students on the path to college*. San Francisco, CA: Jossey-Bass.

Posner, G. J. (2005). *Field experiences: A guide to reflective teaching*. Boston: Pearson.

Sadler, T. D. (2006). I won't last three weeks: Preservice science teachers reflect on their student-teaching experience. *Journal of Science Teacher Education, 17*(3), 217–41.

Schneider, B. (2014). American Education Research Association presidential address: The power of education research for innovation in practice and policy. Paper presented at the American Educational Research Association Annual Meeting, Philadelphia, Pennsylvania, April 5.

Sizer, T. R., & Sizer, N. F. (1999). *The students are watching*. Boston: Beacon.

Thompson, J. G. (2013). *The first-year teacher's survival guide: Ready-to-use strategies, tools, and activities for meeting the challenges of each school day*. San Francisco, CA: Jossey-Bass.

Wong, H. K., & Wong, R. T. (2009). *The first days of school*. Mountain View, CA: Harry K. Wong Publications.

Zeichner, K. (2010). Rethinking the connections between campus courses and field experiences in college- and university-based teacher education. *Journal of Teacher Education, 61*(1–2), 89–99.

NOTE

1. An early version of this chapter appears in *Schools: Studies in education, 13*(2), 339–48.

Conclusion

Similarities between parents and teachers belie and obscure key differences in the process of teaching like a human. Both roles can be enhanced by focusing on qualitative attributes of the lived experience of the child. The bodies of knowledge mined to guide, direct, and nurture child development presuppose properties of sensory firsthand engagement with the world and the multifaceted but hidden work composed from the myriad small, intentional choices that remediate, contour, or retard educational progress; however, the nature of the time-bound, professional responsibilities of teaching can and should define limitations inherent within the distinction between parenting and teaching.

Many service professions, for example, nursing, medicine, clergy, various therapeutic fields, and education, seek to address and accommodate gaps in the progress of the typically developing child. They may also "see a calling" in going above and beyond the role-bound description to help children. "These teachers are as concerned about the kind of person that each student becomes as about how much a student knows" (Bryk, Lee, & Holland, 2005, p. 151). Lortie (1975) underscores the prevalence of teacher-reported "psychic rewards" associated with working with individual students in schools. "When we recall that the culture emphasizes service, we should not be surprised if the data underscore the significance of psychic rewards in the work life of classroom teachers" (p. 103). The emphasis on such satisfaction beyond financial rewards mirrors the meaning-making parents feel from watching the growth and development of their children throughout time.

Jewish tradition has a special word for this feeling, *nachas*, defined as the pride or gratification of the achievements of one's children.

Noddings (2003) calls for parents and teachers to be cooperative educators, both especially responsible for moral or ethical education, responsible for preserving and enhancing caring of and for those they supervise. She speaks of organizing schools for caring, and this book extends and amplifies her construct to suggest the organization of homes for learning. This circle of life connects the arc she has drawn from home to school with one stretching from school to home, acknowledging the vital role of learning that parents can play through the mindful design of real-life authentic engagement with the world through processes of not only teaching and learning, but also listening, dialogue, deep noticing, wondering, inquiring, playing, and imagining alongside children. Yet, it is also crucial to highlight the distinctions between the roles to avoid error, role confusion, or, G-d forbid, inappropriate and unprofessional conduct.

Let's introduce the "supermarket test." If a child unexpectedly sees their teacher in the supermarket, they may nervously hide in an aisle and pretend they have not seen him/her. If one unexpectedly sees a family member in the supermarket, they would generally not seek to avoid the identified party. The point is, while many of the actions and motivations inherent in the relationships are similar, important distinctions are present. Namely, the teacher–student relationship is contextualized by the classroom space. The situated nature of the relationship is housed in the classroom context and limited by time and space of the shared arrangement of circumstance. The formal relationship begins with day one of the school year and ends with the final day of school. While the memories of time shared together live, to greater or lesser degrees, in the minds of the individuals, the formal bonds of connection between the two parties have defined starting and stopping points, clearcut beginnings and endings. This does not mean that teachers refuse all contact and assistance to their students after the school year ends, but in practical terms the nature of the role and relationship in terms of time and effort minimizes at the conclusion of the term limit to make way for the next group of students. Obviously, parenting has no such limitations.

The infinite nature of the parent–child relationship is clearly not contextualized by time and space. In healthy parent–child relationships, love and care exist across time, space, and circumstance. While, in some cases, teachers serve as substitute or surrogate parents, most teachers' emotional attachments to children should not fall into the same type of emotional bond.

Aspects of the work may be similar, but the limitations of teaching ethically, legally, and morally should trace different zones of responsibility, expectation, and attachment. This is not to suggest a clinical or unsympathetic teacher is best to avoid overinvolvement or unhealthy relationship; however, it is evident that the power of teaching is primarily in the classroom space in real time and through memory traces of experience after the formal term has concluded. Nostalgia for both home and school overlay childhood with memories of warmth, fun, and joy—and also pain, sorrow, and humiliation. Experiences can be educative or miseducative in either space. But role-bound responsibilities and obligations anchor parents as the primary guardian, advisor, caretaker, and advocate for the child first and foremost.

Parents can and should complement the educator's contributions to their child's life, but they should never abdicate the role of teacher either. The reverse is not true despite the legal understanding of *in loco parentis*. Understandably, the teacher takes the place of the parent during the school day when the parent is unavailable and is responsible for making wise choices as to the safety, well-being, and overall care of the child during those hours; however, time-bound limitations circumscribe the role. There is no statute of limitations on the parent–child relationship during a lifetime; the parent will always be the parent.

Vivian Gussin Paley (1997) speaks of "narrative continuity." In her classic work *The Girl with the Brown Crayon*, Paley traces her kindergarten class's engagement with Leo Lionni's stories and characters from his illustrated children's books throughout the year. The immersive flow within and around Lionni's many works shapes and punctuates the play, questions, drawing, dancing, and conversation in the classroom environment as the children and teachers make connections between his books and their lives. Schools like to label such connections using jargon like "text-to-self" connections. The sensibility of narrative continuity paints more fluid strokes of authenticity and meaning-making that echo the writing of John Dewey.

> The child's life is an integral, a total one. He passes quickly and readily from one topic to another, as from one spot to another, but is not conscious of transition or break. There is no conscious isolation, hardly conscious distinction. The things that occupy him are held together by the unity of the personal and social interest which his life carries along. Whatever is uppermost in his mind constitutes to him for the time being, the whole universe. (Dewey, 1902/1956, p. 5–6)

Dewey argues that the arbitrary split into subject matter during the school day negates the integrated nature of the world where economics, science, art, and literature merge while children play, build, plant, shop, and craft together. In a similar vein, parents and teachers can deliberately foster the narrative continuity between teaching and learning, talking and listening, and, home and school. Beyond the prosaic "What did you learn in school today?" which devolves dinner conversation into pitiful exercises of awkward and shameful dialogue, parents can discuss current events, promote children's interests outside of school, and open space for children to ask them questions about their jobs and passions. Teachers are professionally reminded by their districts to foster home school connections and practice culturally responsive and sustaining pedagogy. Beyond the jargon, getting to know children means talking about activities and interests outside academic pursuits, letting them share their own expertise and troubles, and allowing them to take healthy risks that nudge skills and needs in positive, forward directions. It is never as simple or mellifluous as it sounds. There is nothing harder in the world, as every individual houses an entire world of hopes and dreams, and disappointments and challenges, and knowledge and questions. The fixation today on fixing education does not mean fixing schools, teachers, parents, or children. The complexity of the task of teaching like a human privileges the complex, uncertain, and vital nature of the roles parents and teachers share.

Paulo Freire (1970/2002, p. 84) describes such praxis as problem-posing dialogic education, which identifies "people as beings aware of their incompletion." His answer to this understanding of humanity and humility, our answer herein, is the transformation from this state of uncertainty to forward-thinking here-and-now pedagogy that takes its point of departure from the people themselves (parents, teachers, and children), with fellowship and solidarity. Teaching like a human means that parents and teachers, within their role-bound, situated contexts, can organize themselves and their lot to discover what can be. "It is important that we take critical ownership of the formation of our selves" (Freire, 2003, p. 59). Teaching like a human assimilates the simultaneous recognition of self and reworking of self in relation to others and the external world. This is a preoccupation worth consideration, construction, and collaboration.

REFERENCES

Bryk, A., Lee, V., & Holland, P. (2005). *Classroom life*. In R. Arum & I. R. Beattie (Eds.), *The structure of schooling: Readings in the sociology of education* (pp. 146–53). Mountain View, CA: Mayfield. (Reprinted from *Catholic Schools and the Common Good*, pp. 81–100, 1993, Harvard University Press.)

Dewey, J. (1902/1956). *The child and the curriculum*. Chicago: University of Chicago Press. (Original work published in 1902.)

Freire, P. (1970/2002). *Pedagogy of the oppressed*, 30th anniversary ed. New York: Continuum.

Freire, P. (2003). Reading the world/reading the word. In *The Jossey-Bass reader on teaching* (pp. 52–61). San Francisco, CA: Jossey-Bass. (Reprinted from *Teachers as cultural workers: Letters to those who dare teach*, 1988.)

Lortie, D. (1975). *Schoolteacher*. Chicago: University of Chicago Press.

Noddings, N. (2003). *Caring: A feminine approach to ethics and moral education*, 2nd ed. Berkeley: University of California Press.

Paley, V. G. (1997). *The girl with the brown crayon*. Cambridge, MA: Harvard University Press.

About the Author

Miriam Hirsch is associate professor of education and chair of the Educator Preparation Program at Stern College for Women, Yeshiva University in New York City, New York. She holds a PhD in Educational Administration, Leadership and Technology from New York University, an MA in Curriculum and Teaching, and an MA in Arts Education from Teachers College, Columbia University. She worked as an elementary school teacher and assistant principal before moving to academia. Her research examines the influence of school stories and narrative inquiry in education. She has published in *Educational Leadership*, *The Teacher Educator*, *The Educational Forum*, *Schools: Studies in Education*, *Teaching Education*, *The Arts and Humanities in Higher Education*, *The Journal of Jewish Education*, and *Jewish Educational Leadership*. *Teach Like a Human: Essays for Parents and Teachers* is her first book. She is the proud mom of five daughters and lives with her husband and family in Passaic, New Jersey.

CPSIA information can be obtained
at www.ICGtesting.com
Printed in the USA
LVHW091906231220
675003LV00005B/31

9 781475 857214